General Instructions

Note *The skill level of these projects is listed as advanced because of the number of small pieces that need to be fitted together. With patience, a confident advanced beginner or intermediate stitcher will probably have no trouble completing these projects.*

1 These projects use plastic canvas in a variety of colors and counts. Most pieces are cut from stiff 7-count plastic canvas for extra durability. Unless instructed otherwise, cut pieces from stiff 7-count plastic canvas.

2 The buildings and other structures of Main Street Village are stitched using a combination of worsted weight (4-ply) yarn and 6-strand cotton embroidery floss. Some instructions call for individual plies of yarn or strands of floss to be removed from the fiber for stitching. In a few cases, doubled fibers are used.

- When stitching with yarn, stitch with a full 4-ply strand unless instructed otherwise.
- When stitching with 6-strand cotton embroidery floss, always separate the individual strands, then recombine the correct number without twisting them before threading your needle.

3 When working embroidery stitches, 1 ply separated from a length of yarn can be substituted for 6 strands of embroidery floss. If you choose to work embroidery stitches with a single ply of yarn, stitch with lengths no longer than 12–18 inches, and handle the fiber gently.

4 Work all French Knots wrapping yarn or floss twice around needle unless instructed otherwise.

5 Use a #18 tapestry needle for stitching on 7-count plastic canvas. Use a #22 needle for stitching on 10- or 14-count plastic canvas.

6 Use a sharp sewing needle and sewing thread whenever instructions call for pieces to be tacked together.

7 Red dashed lines on the graphs indicate where pieces are to be Whipstitched together. Leave these lines unworked as you complete the surrounding background stitches; they will be stitched when the piece is assembled.

White House

Size: 2½ inches W x 4⅛ inches H x 5⅝ inches D
(6.4cm x 10.5cm x 14.4cm)
Skill Level: Advanced

Materials

- Plastic canvas:
    - ½ sheet white 7-count
    - ½ sheet stiff 7-count
- Worsted weight yarn as listed in color key
- 6-strand cotton embroidery floss as listed in color key
- 9 inches (22.9cm) ⅜-inch-wide (1cm) white lace trim
- 2 (¼-inch/0.6cm) round burnt orange wooden beads
- ⅜-inch (1cm) white lace *or* white felt heart motif
- #18 tapestry needle
- Hot-glue gun and glue stick

Stitching Step by Step

1. From white plastic canvas, cut all house walls, porch front wall and side supports according to graphs.

2. From stiff plastic canvas, cut porch front support and porch floor; all stairs, chimney pieces and roof pieces; flower boxes and base according to graphs.

3. Porch front wall and side supports will remain unstitched, as will central area of base. Stitch remaining pieces according to graphs, filling in uncoded areas on walls, porch front support, chimney pieces and stairs with white Continental Stitches and reversing one chimney front/back before you stitch. Leave red dashed lines unworked; these are Whipstitching lines, and will be stitched during assembly. *Note: Around bottom of house, weave rust yarn over and under bars of plastic canvas; the white plastic canvas will resemble grout between the bricks.* Overcast all edges of stairs and base using adjacent colors; Overcast edges of flower boxes with clay and lime green according to graphs.

4. Add embroidery stitches using 6-strand cotton embroidery floss as follows: teal—Straight Stitch around windows and front door; dark gold—Straight Stitch around back door and Backstitch doorknob; French Knot doorknob on front door; red—French Knot flowers on flower boxes.

5. Using lime green yarn, Straight Stitch plants over bricks around bottom of house.

Assembly

1. Using teal yarn throughout, Whipstitch bottom edge of unstitched porch front wall to porch floor, near front edge. Whipstitch long edge of each porch side support to matching edge of porch floor, and Whipstitch one long edge of porch front support to front of porch.

2. Using white yarn throughout, Overcast bottom edge of porch front support; Whipstitch porch front support to porch side supports. Whipstitch back edge of porch to front wall of house. Overcast front and side edges of porch roof; Whipstitch back edge of porch roof to front wall of house.

3. Using white yarn, Overcast top edges of house front, back and side walls; using lime green yarn, Overcast

2 **Main Street Village** • The Needlecraft Shop • Berne, IN 46711 • NeedlecraftShop.com

bottom edges. Using teal and rust yarns according to graphs, Whipstitch house front, side and back walls together.

4 Hot-glue top bar of porch front wall to underside of porch roof, just inside white Overcasting. Center house and porch on base; hot-glue house and porch to base.

5 Using teal yarn throughout, Whipstitch house roof pieces together along one long edge; Overcast remaining edges. Hot-glue roof to house.

6 Using white yarn throughout, Whipstitch chimney front, back and side walls together with top edges even; Overcast remaining edges and edges of chimney top. Center chimney top over chimney; hot-glue in place. Referring to photo, hot-glue chimney to roof.

Finishing

1 Stack front stairs, with the largest on the bottom and all back edges even; hot-glue at front of porch. Repeat with back stairs, hot-gluing them below back door.

2 Cut lace trim to fit inside windows to suggest lace curtains; hot-glue lace to top row of light blue Continental Stitches in each window.

3 Cut lace trim to fit along edges of roof on front of house; hot-glue to roof as shown. Hot-glue lace or felt heart over ends of lace at peak of roof.

4 Hot-glue flower boxes just over bottom edge of larger windows on sides of house.

5 Hot-glue beads on top of chimney as shown to resemble chimney pots.

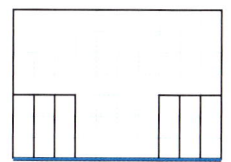

White House Roof
21 holes x 11 holes
Cut 2

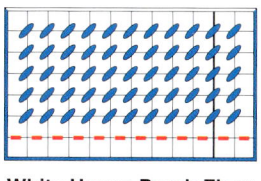

White House Porch Floor
12 holes x 7 holes
Cut 1

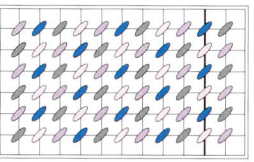

White House Porch Roof
12 holes x 7 holes
Cut 1

White House Porch Front Wall
10 holes x 7 holes
Cut 1 from white plastic canvas,
cut away blue lines;
it will remain unstitched.

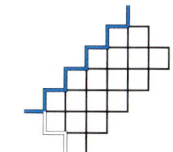

White House Porch Side Support
7 holes x 7 holes
Cut 2 from white plastic canvas;
they will remain unstitched

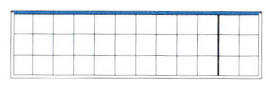

White House Porch Front Support
12 holes x 3 holes
Cut 1

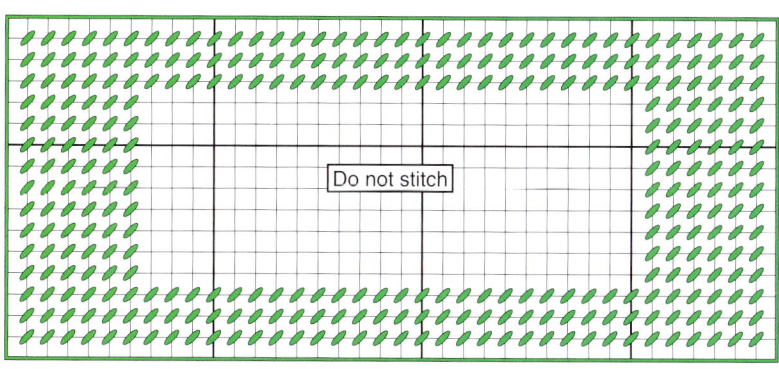

White House Base
37 holes x 16 holes
Cut 1

COLOR KEY	
Yards	**Worsted Weight Yarn**
16 (14.6m)	■ Lime green
14 (12.8m)	■ Teal
6 (5.5m)	■ Clay
6 (5.5m)	■ Rust
5 (4.6m)	□ Rose
5 (4.6m)	■ Lavender
3 (2.7m)	□ Light blue
1 (0.9m)	□ Taupe
1 (0.9m)	■ Aqua
20 (18.3m)	Uncoded areas on all walls, chimney pieces, stairs, and porch front support are White Continental Stitches
	⁄ White Overcasting and Whipstitching
	⁄ Lime green Straight Stitch
	6-strand Embroidery Floss
3 (2.7m)	⁄ Teal Straight Stitch
1 (0.9m)	⁄ Dark gold Straight Stitch
	● Dark gold French Knot
1 (0.9m)	● Red French Knot

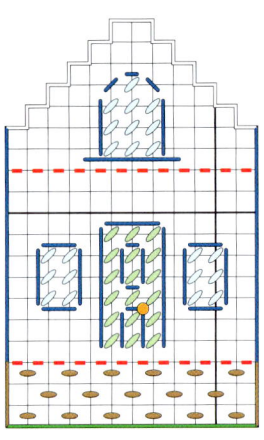

White House Front Wall
12 holes x 19 holes
Cut 1 from white plastic canvas

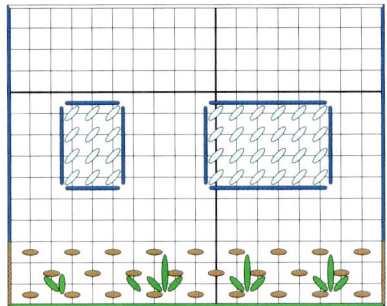

White House Side Wall
18 holes x 14 holes
Cut 2 from white plastic canvas
Stitch one as shown; stitch 1 as mirror image

White House Bottom Back Stair
1 holes x 4 holes
Cut 1

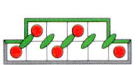

White House Flower Box
6 holes x 2 holes
Cut 2

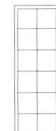

White House Middle Front Stair
2 holes x 6 holes
Cut 1

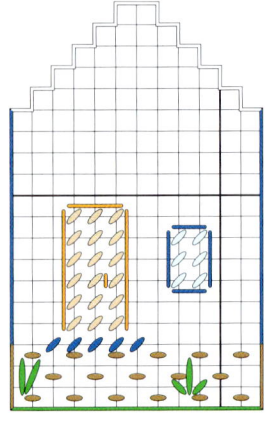

White House Back Wall
12 holes x 19 holes
Cut 1 from white plastic canvas

White House Chimney Short Side
3 holes x 2 holes
Cut 1

White House Bottom Front Stair
1 holes x 6 holes
Cut 1

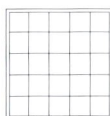

White House Chimney Top
5 holes x 5 holes
Cut 1

White House Top Back Stair
3 holes x 4 holes
Cut 1

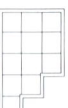

White House Chimney Front/Back
3 holes x 5 holes
Cut 2, reversing 1 before stitching

White House Middle Back Stair
2 holes x 4 holes
Cut 1

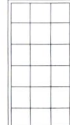

White House Chimney Long Side
3 holes x 6 holes
Cut 1

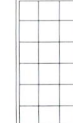

White House Top Front Stair
3 holes x 6 holes
Cut 1

COLOR KEY		
Yards		Worsted Weight Yarn
16 (14.6m)	■	Lime green
14 (12.8m)	■	Teal
6 (5.5m)	■	Clay
6 (5.5m)	■	Rust
5 (4.6m)	■	Rose
5 (4.6m)	■	Lavender
3 (2.7m)	■	Light blue
1 (0.9m)	■	Taupe
1 (0.9m)	■	Aqua
20 (18.3m)		Uncoded areas on all walls, chimney pieces, stairs, and porch front support are White Continental Stitches
	╱	White Overcasting and Whipstitching
	╱	Lime green Straight Stitch
		6-strand Embroidery Floss
3 (2.7m)	╱	Teal Straight Stitch
1 (0.9m)	╱	Dark gold Straight Stitch
	●	Dark gold French Knot
1 (0.9m)	●	Red French Knot

4 *Main Street Village* • The Needlecraft Shop • Berne, IN 46711 • NeedlecraftShop.com

Pink House

Size: 3¾ inches W x 4¾ inches H x 3 inches D
(9.5cm x 12.1cm x 7.6cm)
Skill Level: Advanced

Materials
- Plastic canvas:
    - 1 sheet stiff 7-count
    - Scraps of white 7-count
    - Scraps of clear 14-count
- Worsted weight yarn as listed in color key
- 6-strand cotton embroidery floss as listed in color key
- 7 inches (17.8cm) ¼-inch-wide (0.6cm) white Venice lace trim with ½-inch-wide (1.3cm) motifs
- 2 (1-inch/2.5cm) pieces 3mm green chenille stem
- 2 (¼-inch/0.6cm) green round beads
- Royal blue sewing thread
- Tapestry needles: #18 and #22
- Sewing needle
- Hot-glue gun and glue stick

Stitching Step by Step

1 From stiff plastic canvas, cut all house and turret walls; all roof pieces, including dormers and gables; and base according to graphs.

2 From white plastic canvas, cut porch side and porch front according to graphs.

3 From 14-count plastic canvas, cut welcome mat according to graph. Using 6 strands light yellow embroidery floss, fill in with Continental Stitches, Overcasting edges as you stitch.

4 Stitch one turret front/side wall according to graph for front, filling in uncoded areas with pink Continental Stitches; fill in second piece completely with pink Continental Stitches for side.

5 On remaining pieces, fill in uncoded areas on walls with pink Continental Stitches; fill in uncoded areas on all roof, dormer and gable pieces with royal blue Continental Stitches. Porch front and porch side will remain unstitched, as will much of the base. Leave red dashed lines unworked; these are Whipstitching lines, and will be stitched during assembly. As you stitch, Overcast edges of gray stoop and camel porch floor on base, using adjacent colors.

6 Add embroidery stitches using 6-strand cotton embroidery floss as follows: white—Backstitch and Straight Stitch around smaller light aqua windows and around sides and tops of both doors; light yellow—French Knot doorknobs on front and back doors.

7 Using black embroidery floss throughout, add additional details: 1 strand—Backstitch and

Straight Stitch "stained glass" frames around first-floor picture windows, and windows in front and back doors; 3 strands—Backstitch words on welcome mat; 6 strands—Backstitch hinges on doors.

8 Using grass green yarn, Straight Stitch plants along bottom of back and left side walls.

Assembly

1 Using royal blue yarn throughout, Overcast sides and front edge of porch roof between arrows; Whipstitch back edge of roof to house's front wall.

2 Using camel yarn, Whipstitch bottom edge of unstitched porch front and porch side support to edges of porch floor, matching corners carefully at front corner of base.

3 Using pink yarn, Whipstitch turret front and side walls and house front wall to base. Using grass green yarn, Whipstitch house side and back walls to edges of base.

4 Using pink yarn throughout, Whipstitch turret back wall to turret side wall and house left side wall, with top edges of all walls even. Whipstitch remaining walls together at corners.

5 Overcast top edges of house and turret using pink and royal blue yarns according to graphs.

6 Using sewing needle and blue thread, tack unstitched porch front and side supports to underside of porch roof (five or six stitches are sufficient).

7 Using royal blue yarn throughout, Whipstitch turret roof sections together in a square cone; Overcast edges. Whipstitch turret window gable pieces together along one short edge; Overcast remaining edges. Repeat with front door gable. Whipstitch dormer pieces together along one straight edge so that diagonal edges will fit in cutout on house front roof; Overcast remaining edges. Whipstitch house front roof and back roof together along matching straight edges; Overcast remaining edges.

8 Position main roof on house so that notches slide between dormer and turret; hot-glue in place. Hot-glue dormer over notch in roof.

9 Hot-glue turret roof, window and front door gables in place as shown.

Finishing

1 Cut five motifs from lace trim. Hot-glue one at top of turret; one at top of each tall light aqua window on front of house; and one at highest point on each side of house.

2 Hot-glue additional lace trim across top edge of roof.

3 Hot-glue welcome mat to front stoop.

4 Bend each piece of chenille stem into a topiary-style spiral: Wind chenille around needle two or three times, then pull end gently to extend coils. Hot-glue straight end in bead for pot. Hot-glue beads to front stoop, beside door.

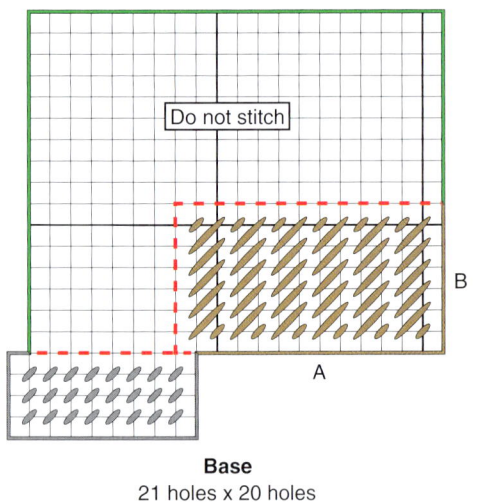

Base
21 holes x 20 holes
Cut 1

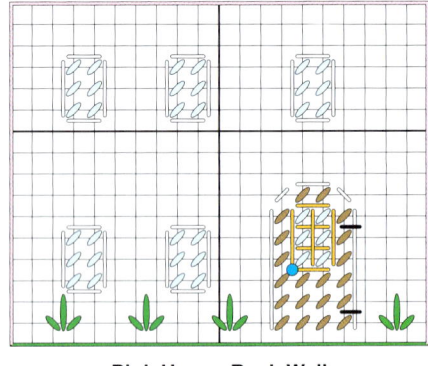

Pink House Front Wall
13 holes x 18 holes
Cut 1

Pink House Back Wall
20 holes x 16 holes
Cut 1

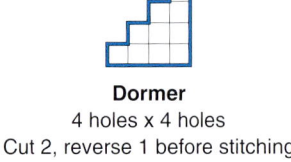

Dormer
4 holes x 4 holes
Cut 2, reverse 1 before stitching

Front Door Gable
5 holes x 2 holes
Cut 2

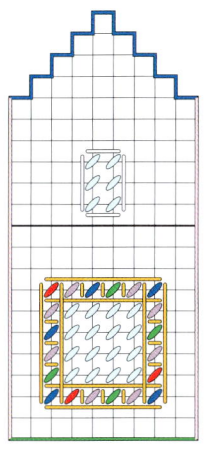

Pink House Right Side Wall
9 holes x 20 holes
Cut 1

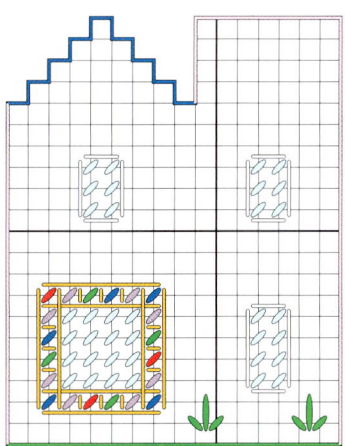

Pink House Left Side Wall
16 holes x 20 holes
Cut 1

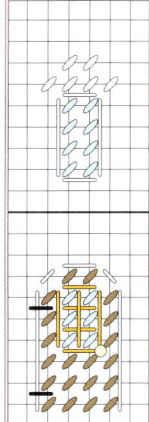

Turret Front/Side Wall
7 holes x 20 holes
Cut 2
Stitch 1 as shown for front;
stitch 1 completely in pink
Continental Stitches for side

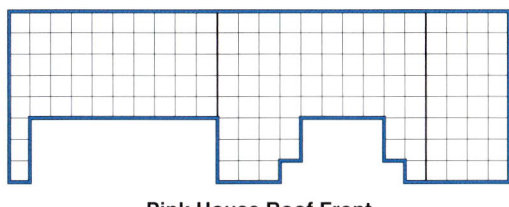

Pink House Roof Front
24 holes x 8 holes
Cut 1

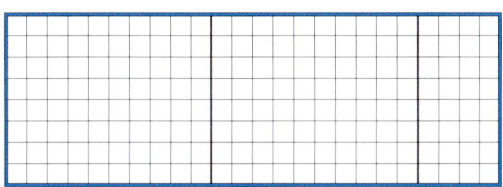

Pink House Roof Back
24 holes x 8 holes
Cut 1

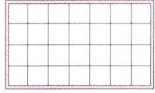

Turret Back Wall
7 holes x 4 holes
Cut 1

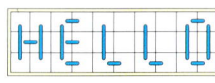

Welcome Mat
10 holes x 3 holes
Cut 1 from 14-count plastic canvas

Turret Window Gable
3 holes x 2 holes
Cut 2

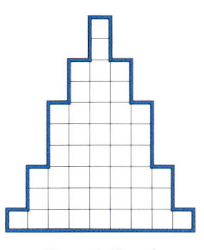

Turret Roof
9 holes x 10 holes
Cut 4

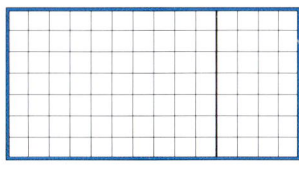

Porch Roof
14 holes x 7 holes
Cut 1

COLOR KEY	
Yards	**Worsted Weight Yarn**
18 (16.5m)	■ Royal blue
4 (3.7m)	□ Light aqua
3 (2.7m)	■ Camel
3 (2.7m)	■ Grass green
2 (1.8m)	■ Cornflower blue
1 (0.9m)	■ Gray
25 (22.9m)	Uncoded areas on all walls are Pink Continental Stitch
	Uncoded areas on all roof, gable and dormer pieces are royal blue Continental Stitches
	╱ Pink Whipstitching
	╱ Grass green Straight Stitch
	6-strand Embroidery Floss
1 (0.9m)	Uncoded areas on welcome mat are light yellow Continental Stitches
	╱ Light yellow Overcasting
3 (2.7m)	╱ White Straight Stitch
1 (0.9m)	╱ Black (1-strand) Backstitch and Straight Stitch
	╱ Black (3-strand) Backstitch and Straight Stitch
	╱ Black (6-strand) Backstitch and Straight Stitch
	○ Light yellow French Knot

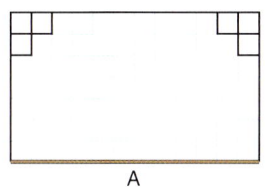

A
Porch Front
12 holes x 7 holes
Cut 1 from white plastic canvas;
cut away blue lines

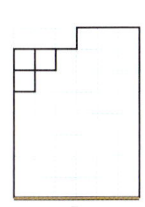

B
Porch Side
6 holes x 8 holes
Cut 1 from white plastic canvas;
cut away blue lines

Blue House

Size: 4½ inches W x 3⅛ inches H x 2½ inches D
(11.4cm x 7.9cm x 6.4cm)
Skill Level: Advanced

Materials
- Plastic canvas:
    - 1 sheet stiff 7-count
    - Scrap of white 7-count
- Worsted weight yarn as listed in color key
- 6-strand cotton embroidery floss as listed in color key
- 6 motifs approximately ¼ inch (0.6m) square cut from white Venice lace
- 2 (4mm) opaque white faceted beads
- #18 tapestry needle
- Hot-glue gun and glue stick

Stitching Step by Step

1 From stiff plastic canvas, cut all house walls; all chimney pieces; porch roof and house roof pieces; base and flower boxes according to graphs.

2 From white plastic canvas, cut porch front and side walls according to graphs.

3 Stitch porch front according to graph, Whipstitching sides to front with dark terra cotta and white yarns and Overcasting top edges of front with white yarn as you stitch.

4 Stitch remaining pieces according to graphs, leaving portion of base unstitched and filling in uncoded areas on remaining pieces with light blue Continental Stitches. Leave red dashed lines unworked; these are Whipstitching lines, and will be stitched during assembly. Overcast edges of flower boxes with light kelly green and light terra cotta according to graphs as you stitch.

5 Using white yarn throughout, Backstitch and Straight Stitch around upper-story windows; Straight Stitch over top of door, and details on front and back walls.

6 Add embroidery stitches using 6-strand cotton embroidery floss as follows: black—Straight Stitch across tops of first-story windows; white—Straight Stitch around door; gold—French Knot doorknob; red—French Knot flowers on flower boxes.

Assembly

1 Center and hot-glue lace motif over each first-story window. Hot-glue flower boxes below each first-story window.

2 Using gray yarn, Overcast side and front edges of porch roof; using white yarn throughout, Whipstitch back edge of porch roof to house front wall; Whipstitch bottom edge of house front wall to base.

3 Using light blue yarn, Whipstitch porch side walls to house front wall. Hot-glue porch roof to top edges of porch front and side walls.

4 Using dark kelly green, Whipstitch bottom edges of porch and remaining house walls to base. Using white yarn throughout, Whipstitch house walls together along corners sides and front edge of porch roof between arrows; Whipstitch back edge of roof to house's front wall. Overcast top edges of house.

5 Using gray yarn throughout, Whipstitch house roof pieces together along one short edge; Overcast remaining edges. Hot-glue roof to house.

6 Using dark terra cotta yarn throughout, Whipstitch chimney front, back and side walls together with top edges even; Overcast remaining edges. Referring to photo, hot-glue chimney to roof.

Finishing

Hot-glue beads to vertical posts extending from top of front porch railing.

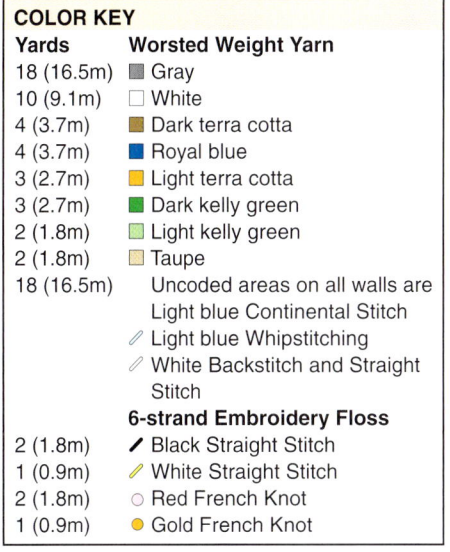

COLOR KEY	
Yards	**Worsted Weight Yarn**
18 (16.5m)	■ Gray
10 (9.1m)	□ White
4 (3.7m)	■ Dark terra cotta
4 (3.7m)	■ Royal blue
3 (2.7m)	■ Light terra cotta
3 (2.7m)	■ Dark kelly green
2 (1.8m)	■ Light kelly green
2 (1.8m)	■ Taupe
18 (16.5m)	Uncoded areas on all walls are Light blue Continental Stitch
	╱ Light blue Whipstitching
	╱ White Backstitch and Straight Stitch
6-strand Embroidery Floss	
2 (1.8m)	╱ Black Straight Stitch
1 (0.9m)	╱ White Straight Stitch
2 (1.8m)	○ Red French Knot
1 (0.9m)	● Gold French Knot

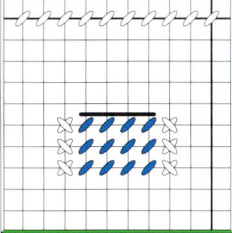

Blue House Side Wall
11 holes x 11 holes
Cut 2

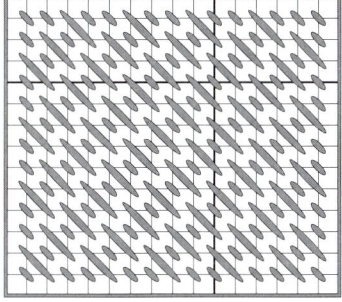

Blue House Roof
16 holes x 14 holes
Cut 2

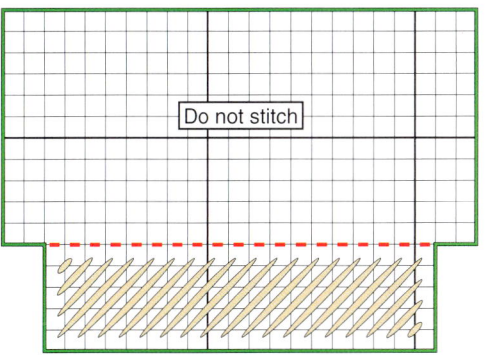

Blue House Base
23 holes x 16 holes
Cut 1

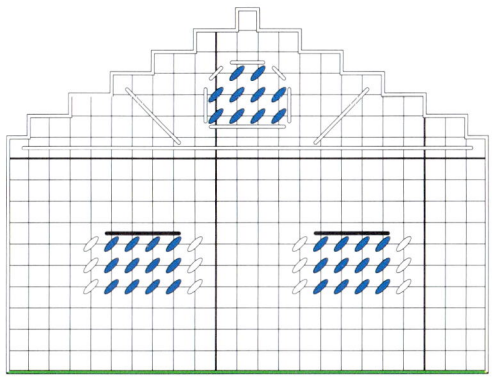

Blue House Back Wall
23 holes x 17 holes
Cut 1

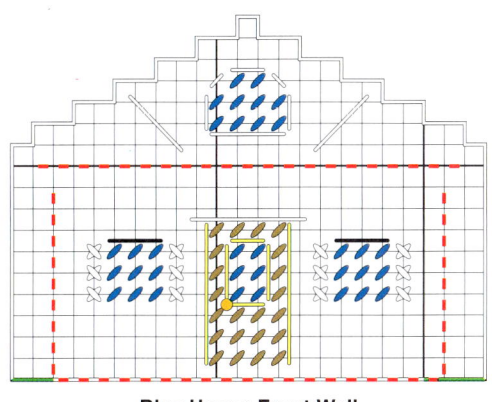

Blue House Front Wall
23 holes x 17 holes
Cut 1

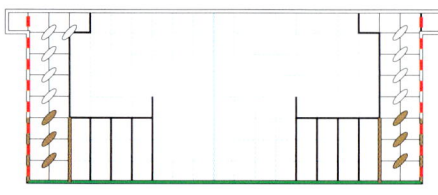

Blue House Porch Front Wall
21 holes x 8 holes
Cut 1 from white plastic canvas;
cut away blue lines

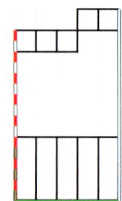

Blue House Porch Side Wall
5 holes x 9 holes
Cut 2 from white plastic canvas;
cut away blue lines

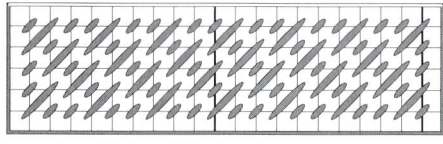

Blue House Porch Roof
21 holes x 6 holes
Cut 1

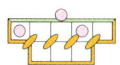

Flower Box
5 holes x 2 holes
Cut 6

Blue House Chimney Short Side
2 holes x 3 holes
Cut 1

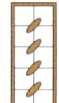

Blue House Chimney Long Side
2 holes x 5 holes
Cut 1

Blue House Chimney Front/Back
2 holes x 4 holes
Cut 2

COLOR KEY

Yards	Worsted Weight Yarn
18 (16.5m)	■ Gray
10 (9.1m)	□ White
4 (3.7m)	■ Dark terra cotta
4 (3.7m)	■ Royal blue
3 (2.7m)	■ Light terra cotta
3 (2.7m)	■ Dark kelly green
2 (1.8m)	■ Light kelly green
2 (1.8m)	□ Taupe
18 (16.5m)	Uncoded areas on all walls are Light blue Continental Stitch
	∕ Light blue Whipstitching
	∕ White Backstitch and Straight Stitch

6-strand Embroidery Floss

2 (1.8m)	∕ Black Straight Stitch
1 (0.9m)	∕ White Straight Stitch
2 (1.8m)	○ Red French Knot
1 (0.9m)	● Gold French Knot

Yellow House

Size: 3¼ inches W x 4 inches H x 3¼ inches D (8.2cm x 10.2cm x 8.2cm)
Skill Level: Advanced

Materials

- Plastic canvas:
    - ½ sheet stiff 7-count
    - ½ sheet light yellow 7-count
- Worsted weight yarn as listed in color key
- 6-strand cotton embroidery floss as listed in color key
- Light yellow sewing thread
- #18 tapestry needle
- Sewing needle
- Hot-glue gun and glue stick

Stitching Step by Step

1 From stiff plastic canvas, cut yellow house walls 3 and 4, porch walls 1 and 2; all bay window pieces; all chimney pieces; all roof pieces and base according to graphs.

2 From light yellow plastic canvas, cut two yellow house roof trim pieces and house walls 1 and 2 according to graphs.

3 The roof trim pieces and portions of house walls 1 and 2 and the base will remain unstitched. Stitch all remaining pieces according to graphs, filling in uncoded areas with light yellow Continental Stitches, and reversing one chimney front/back piece, one inner roof and one outer roof before you stitch. Leave red dashed lines unworked; these are Whipstitching lines, and will be stitched during assembly. Overcast edges of porch using light gray as you stitch.

4 Add embroidery stitches using yarn as follows: dark terra cotta—Straight Stitch shutters; kelly green—Straight Stitch flower foliage.

5 Add embroidery stitches using 6-strand cotton embroidery floss as follows: black—Backstitch and Straight Stitch doors; gold—French Knot doorknobs, Straight Stitch over and under windows, and Straight Stitch around narrow windows on bay window sides; orange—French Knot flowers on house walls.

Assembly

1 Using light yellow yarn, Whipstitch a bay window side to each side of bay window front. Bend sides back slightly to match diagonal edges on bay window top and bottom; Whipstitch top and bottom to assembled front and sides. Overcast all remaining edges.

2 Using light gray yarn throughout, Whipstitch the bottom edge of porch wall 1 to the base along the left edge of the light gray porch floor where indicated by numeral 1; Whipstitch porch wall 2 along the other edge of the porch floor where indicated by numeral 2.

3 Whipstitch the bottom edges of house walls 1 and 2 to the front and right side edges of the base where indicated by numerals 3 and 4, matching unstitched porch posts at the outer corner of the porch floor; use light gray yarn adjacent to the porch, and kelly green along all other edges.

4 Using kelly green yarn, Whipstitch the bottom edges of house walls 3 and 4 to the left side and back edges of the base respectively, where indicated by numerals 6 and 5.

5 Using gold yarn throughout, Whipstitch porch walls together along inside corner. Whipstitch all other walls together along corners, and Overcast across top edges. On porch, Overcast across the top edge of the unstitched porch supports; where porch posts meet, Whipstitch them together only through the top pair of holes.

6 Hot-glue porch roof over porch.

7 Using dark gray yarn throughout, loosely Whipstitch inside roof pieces together along diagonal edges to form a right angle, right sides facing. Loosely Whipstitch outside roof pieces together along diagonal edges to form a right angle, wrong sides facing.

8 Whipstitch inner and outer roof halves together, wrong sides facing, along straight edges to form roof; Overcast edges.

9 Using sewing needle and light yellow thread, tack unstitched roof trim pieces across top ridge of roof. Hot-glue roof to house.

10 Using dark terra cotta yarn throughout, Whipstitch chimney front, back and side walls together with top edges even; Overcast remaining edges. Referring to photo, hot-glue chimney to roof.

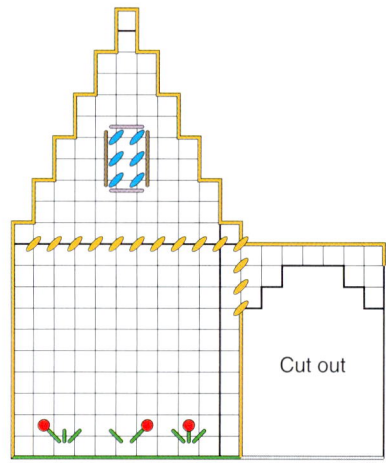

Yellow House Wall 1
18 holes x 21 holes
Cut 1 from light yellow plastic canvas;
porch area at right should remain unstitched

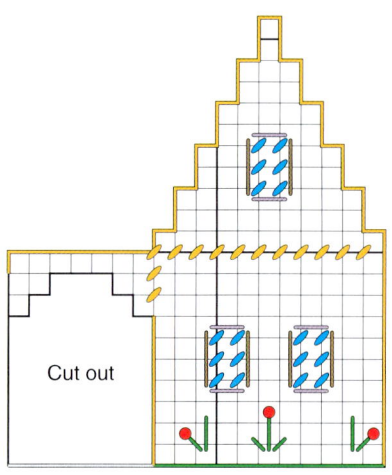

Yellow House Wall 2
18 holes x 21 holes
Cut 1 from light yellow plastic canvas;
porch area at left should remain unstitched

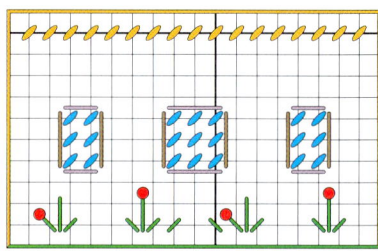

Yellow House Wall 3
18 holes x 11 holes
Cut 1

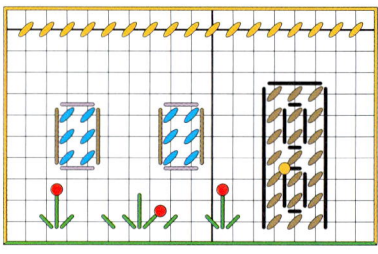

Yellow House Wall 4
18 holes x 11 holes
Cut 1

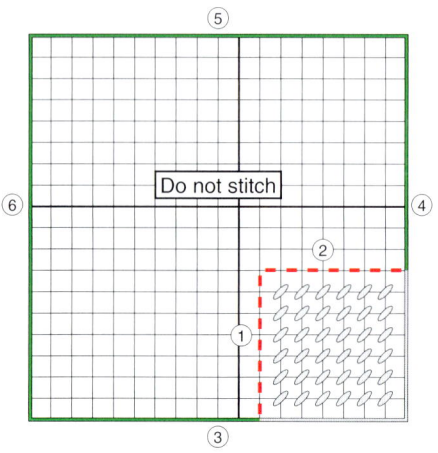

Yellow House Base
18 holes x 18 holes
Cut 1

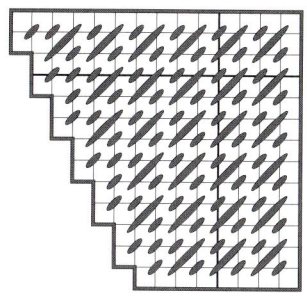

Yellow House Inner Roof
14 holes x 13 holes
Cut 2; reverse 1 before stitching

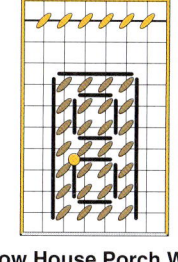

Yellow House Porch Wall 1
7 holes x 11 holes
Cut 1

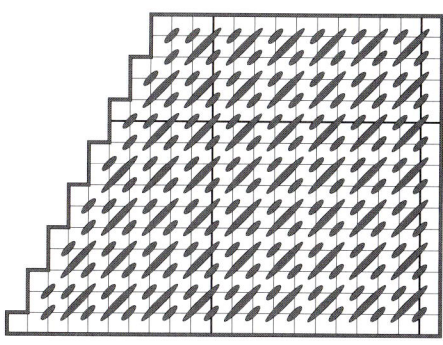

Yellow House Outer Roof
21 holes x 15 holes
Cut 2; reverse 1 before stitching

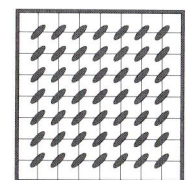

Yellow House Porch Roof
8 holes x 8 holes
Cut 1

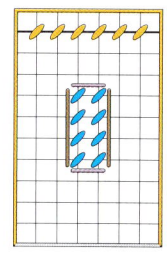

Yellow House Porch Wall 2
7 holes x 11 holes
Cut 1

Yellow House Roof Trim
14 holes x 2 holes
Cut 2 from light yellow plastic canvas;
they will remain unstitched

Yellow House Chimney Short Side
2 holes x 3 holes
Cut 1

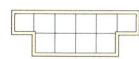
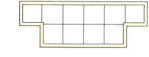

Bay Window Top/Bottom
6 holes x 2 holes
Cut 2

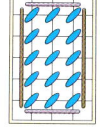

Bay Window Front
4 holes x 6 holes
Cut 1

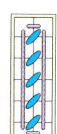

Bay Window Side
2 holes x 6 holes
Cut 2

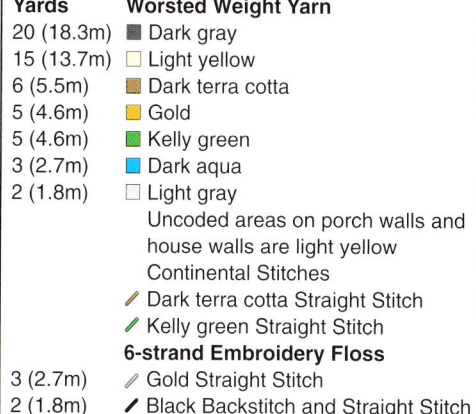

COLOR KEY		
Yards		**Worsted Weight Yarn**
20 (18.3m)	■	Dark gray
15 (13.7m)	□	Light yellow
6 (5.5m)	■	Dark terra cotta
5 (4.6m)	■	Gold
5 (4.6m)	■	Kelly green
3 (2.7m)	■	Dark aqua
2 (1.8m)	□	Light gray
		Uncoded areas on porch walls and house walls are light yellow Continental Stitches
	╱	Dark terra cotta Straight Stitch
	╱	Kelly green Straight Stitch
		6-strand Embroidery Floss
3 (2.7m)	╱	Gold Straight Stitch
2 (1.8m)	╱	Black Backstitch and Straight Stitch
2 (1.8m)	●	Orange French Knot
2 (1.8m)	●	Gold French Knot

Yellow House Chimney Front/Back
2 holes x 7 holes
Cut 2; reverse 1 before stitching

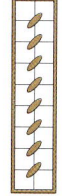

Yellow House Chimney Long Side
2 holes x 9 holes
Cut 1

The Needlecraft Shop • Berne, IN 46711 • NeedlecraftShop.com • **Main Street Village 13**

Green House

Size: 3¼ inches W x 3¾ inches H x 3¼ inches D (8.2cm x 9.5cm x 8.2cm)

Skill Level: Advanced

Materials

- ❏ 1 sheet stiff 7-count plastic canvas
- ❏ Worsted weight yarn as listed in color key
- ❏ 6-strand cotton embroidery floss as listed in color key
- ❏ 2 (3-inch/7.6cm) pieces 20-gauge wire
- ❏ #18 tapestry needle
- ❏ Hot-glue gun and glue stick

Stitching Step by Step

1 From stiff plastic canvas, cut all pieces according to graphs.

2 Using taupe yarn according to graph, stitch the entryway roof/right side, holding 20-gauge wire on underside along rows indicated on graph and catching wire under your stitches. While stitching, allow the wire ends to extend beyond edges of plastic canvas; when stitching is complete, clip wire ends even with plastic canvas.

3 The base will remain unstitched. Stitch all remaining pieces according to graphs, filling in uncoded areas with spring green Continental Stitches, and reversing one chimney front/back piece before you stitch. On shutters, Overcast short edges and one long edge of each shutter. Leave red dashed lines unworked; these are Whipstitching lines, and will be stitched during assembly.

4 Add embroidery stitches using yarn as follows: avocado—Straight Stitch and Backstitch wall details and windowsills of front entryway window and shuttered windows; taupe—Straight Stitch windowsills on remaining windows; hunter green—Straight Stitch flower foliage around house.

5 Add embroidery stitches using 6-strand cotton embroidery floss as follows: black—Backstitch and Straight Stitch door; bright pink—French Knot flowers on house and entryway walls; avocado— Backstitch and Straight Stitch details on windows.

Assembly

1 Using taupe yarn throughout, Whipstitch shutters to side walls beside windows.

2 Using avocado yarn throughout, Whipstitch left edge of entryway tall side wall to house front wall near left edge. Whipstitch right edge of entryway short wall to house front wall near right edge where indicated.

3 Using hunter green throughout, Whipstitch bottom edges of house entryway and walls to base.

4 Using avocado yarn throughout, Whipstitch walls together at corners, working from bottom up; Overcast top edges.

14 Main Street Village • The Needlecraft Shop • Berne, IN 46711 • NeedlecraftShop.com

5 Using taupe yarn throughout, Whipstitch roof front and back together along long straight edge; Overcast remaining edges. Whipstitch entryway roof pieces together along matching shorter edges; Overcast remaining edges.

6 Hot-glue roof to house with notch fitting around entryway; hot-glue entryway roof to main roof and entryway, bending the longer side to fit curve of entryway front wall.

7 Using light terra cotta yarn throughout, Whipstitch chimney front, back and side walls together with top edges even; Overcast remaining edges. Referring to photo, hot-glue chimney to roof.

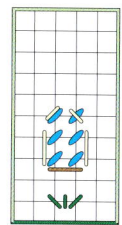

Entryway Tall Side Wall
5 holes x 10 holes
Cut 1

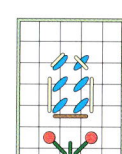

Entryway Short Side Wall
5 holes x 7 holes
Cut 1

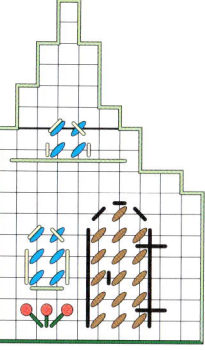

Entryway Front Wall
10 holes x 16 holes
Cut 1

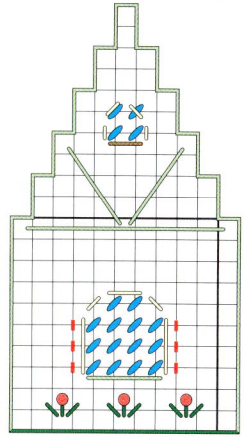

Green House Side Wall
11 holes x 20 holes
Cut 2

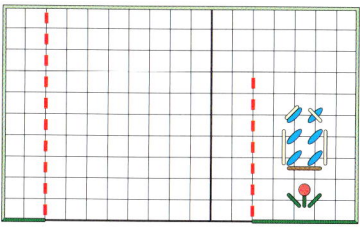

Green House Front Wall
17 holes x 10 holes
Cut 1

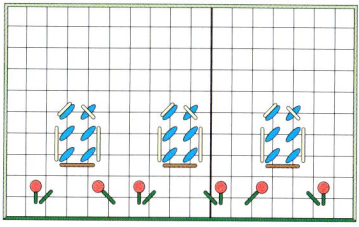

Green House Back Wall
17 holes x 10 holes
Cut 1

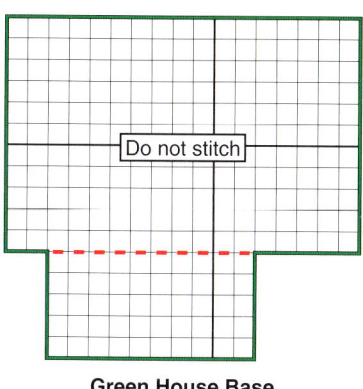

Green House Base
17 holes x 16 holes
Cut 1

COLOR KEY	
Yards	**Worsted Weight Yarn**
24 (21.9m)	■ Taupe
10 (9.1m)	■ Avocado green
3 (2.7m)	■ Dark aqua
2 (1.8m)	■ Light terra cotta
18 (16.5m)	Uncoded areas on walls are spring green Continental Stitch
4 (3.7m)	╱ Hunter green Whipstitch and Straight Stitch
	╱ Taupe Straight Stitch
	╱ Avocado green Straight Stitch
3 (2.7m)	**6-strand Embroidery Floss**
	╱ Avocado green Backstitch and Straight Stitch
2 (1.8m)	
1 (0.9m)	● Bright pink French Knot
	╱ Black Backstitch and Straight Stitch

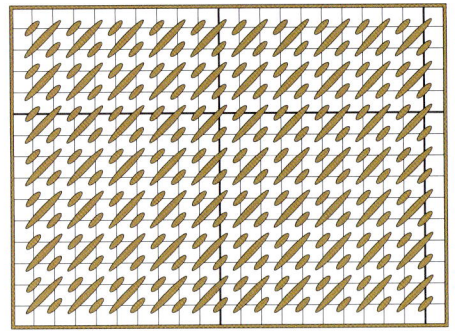

Green House Roof Back
21 holes x 15 holes
Cut 1

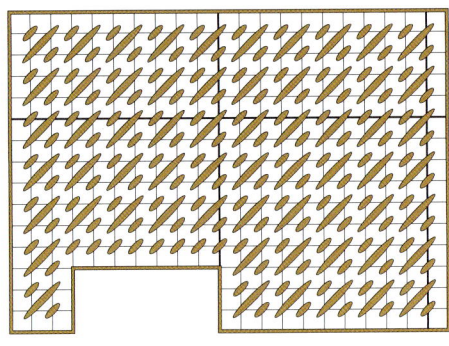

Green House Roof Front
21 holes x 15 holes
Cut 1

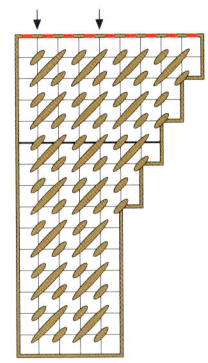

Entryway Roof/Right Side
9 holes x 15 holes
Cut 1

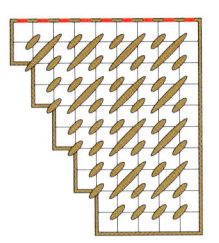

Entryway Roof/Left Side
9 holes x 10 holes
Cut 1

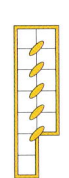

Green House Chimney Front/Back
2 holes x 7 holes
Cut 2; reverse 1 before stitching

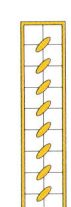

Green House Chimney Long Side
2 holes x 9 holes
Cut 1

Green House Chimney Short Side
2 holes x 3 holes
Cut 1

Green House Shutter
1 hole x 3 holes
Cut 4

COLOR KEY

Yards	Worsted Weight Yarn
24 (21.9m)	■ Taupe
10 (9.1m)	■ Avocado green
3 (2.7m)	■ Dark aqua
2 (1.8m)	■ Light terra cotta
18 (16.5m)	Uncoded areas on walls are spring green Continental Stitch
4 (3.7m)	╱ Hunter green Whipstitch and Straight Stitch
	╱ Taupe Straight Stitch
	╱ Avocado green Straight Stitch
3 (2.7m)	**6-strand Embroidery Floss**
	╱ Avocado green Backstitch and Straight Stitch
2 (1.8m)	
1 (0.9m)	● Bright pink French Knot
	╱ Black Backstitch and Straight Stitch

16 *Main Street Village* • *The Needlecraft Shop* • *Berne, IN 46711* • *NeedlecraftShop.com*

Leafy Trees

Size: 2 inches diameter x approximately 3½ inches H (5.1cm x 8.9cm)
Skill Level: Beginner

Materials

- Small amount stiff plastic canvas
- 4 yards (3.7m) worsted weight yarn in desired color for ground
- 4½ inches (11.4cm) curly chenille in desired color for leaves
- 12-inch (30.5cm) chenille stem in desired color for tree trunk
- Size 18 tapestry needle
- Hot-glue gun and glue stick

Stitching Step by Step

1 Cut leafy tree base according to graph. Using selected yarn, fill in base with Continental Stitches and Overcast edges.

2 Cut chenille stem into three 4-inch (10.2cm) pieces. Hold pieces together, staggering ends so that each is ¼ inch (0.6cm) from the next.

3 Pinch chenille stems together 1½ inches (3.8cm) from top of tallest piece. Twist stems together four or five times to form trunk 1¼–1½ inches (3.2cm–3.8cm) in length.

4 Push individual bottom ends of chenille pieces through separate holes indicated on graph, from right side to wrong side of plastic canvas until twisted trunk is within ¼ inch (0.6cm) of base.

5 Turn base over. Flatten ends of chenille stems against base as flat as possible, pointing them in different directions. Trim any ends that protrude beyond base.

6 Separate chenille stems above trunk and arrange them into natural-looking branches, reaching upward.

7 Cut curly chenille into three 1½-inch (3.8cm) pieces. Twist the wire in each piece into a ring so that the chenille piece looks like a ball.

8 Hot-glue one piece of curly chenille to the top of each chenille branch.

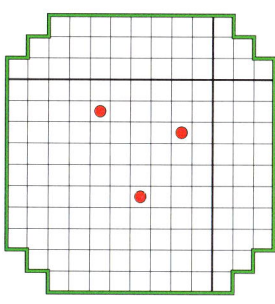

Leafy Tree Base
13 holes x 13 holes
Cut 1 for each

COLOR KEY	
Yards	**Worsted Weight Yarn**
4 (3.6m)	Work uncoded areas in Continental Stitches and Overcast using any ground color
●	Thread chenille roots through base

Grouped Fir Trees

Size: 1¾ inches W x 1 inch D (4.4cm x 2.5cm)
Skill Level: Beginner

Materials

- Small amount stiff plastic canvas
- 3 yards (2.7m) worsted weight yarn in desired color for ground
- 3 inches (7.6cm) bumpy chenille (2 or 3 bumps) in any shade of green
- Size 18 tapestry needle
- Hot-glue gun and glue stick

Stitching Step by Step

1 Cut fir trees base according to graph. Using selected yarn, fill in base with Continental Stitches and Overcast edges.

2 Cut chenille bumps into tree shapes:
Small trees: Cut bumps in half, then cut down pieces and trim tapered ends to make trees ranging in height from ½–1½ inches (1.3cm–3.8cm).

Three taller trees: Taper individual bumps to make trees ranging in height from 1½–2 inches (3.8cm–5cm).

3 Arrange trees on bases in natural-looking groups of three or four. Hot-glue bottoms of trees to stitched tree base.

Fir Trees Base
11 holes x 7 holes
Cut 1 for each group

COLOR KEY	
Yards	**Worsted Weight Yarn**
4 (3.6m)	Work uncoded areas in Continental Stitches and Overcast using any ground color

Potted Fir Trees

Size: 1 inch W x 1 inch D (2.5cm x 2.5cm)
Skill Level: Beginner

Materials

- Small amount stiff plastic canvas
- 2 yards (1.8m) worsted weight yarn in desired color for ground
- 3-inch (7.6cm) "bump" of bumpy chenille in any shade of green
- Metallic, glass or plastic bead, up to 1½ inches (3.8cm) tall and ⅝ inch (1.7cm) diameter
- Size 18 tapestry needle
- Hot-glue gun and glue stick

Stitching Step by Step

1 Cut potted fir tree base according to graph. Using selected yarn, fill in base with Continental Stitches and Overcast edges.

2 Trim chenille bump to about 2 inches (5.1cm). Insert broad end into bead; push chenille through bead until what remains looks like a little fir tree. (You may need to trim the top a bit to achieve this effect.) Then pull it up slightly so that the bottom of the tree looks natural, not crimped. Cut off any chenille protruding from bottom of bead.

3 Hot-glue bead in center of stitched tree base.

Potted Fir Tree Base
7 holes x 7 holes
Cut 1

COLOR KEY	
Yards	**Worsted Weight Yarn**
2 (1.8m)	Work uncoded areas in Continental Stitches and Overcast using any ground color

City Gates

Size: 3 inches W x 2 inches H x 1¼ inches D
(7.6cm x 5.1cm x 3.2cm)
Skill Level: Intermediate

Materials

❑ Plastic canvas:
  ½ sheet stiff 7-count
  Small amount 10-count
❑ Worsted weight yarn as listed in color key
❑ 6-strand cotton embroidery floss as listed in color key
❑ Green pompoms:
  3 (¼-inch/0.6cm)
  4 (5mm)
  2 (3mm)
❑ 2 (½-inch/1.3cm) wooden balls
❑ Ivory craft paint
❑ Paintbrush
❑ Tapestry needles: #18 and #22
❑ Hot-glue gun and glue stick

Stitching Step by Step

1 From stiff plastic canvas, cut bases, walls, wall caps, posts and post caps according to graphs.

2 From 10-count plastic canvas, cut signs according to graphs.

3 Stitch bases, posts, wall caps and post caps according to graphs. Leave red dashed lines unworked; these

are Whipstitching lines, and will be stitched during assembly. Leave areas inside Whipstitching lines on bases unstitched as well. Overcast bases, wall caps and post caps using adjacent colors.

4 Stitch two walls according to graph for wall fronts, filling in uncoded areas with light terra cotta Continental Stitches. Stitch remaining two walls completely with light terra cotta Continental Stitches for wall backs.

5 Using 12 strands ivory embroidery floss, fill in uncoded areas of signs with Continental Stitches; Overcast edges.

6 Add embroidery stitches using floss as follows: black—Backstitch lettering on signs; ivory—Straight Stitch outlines on wall fronts.

Assembly

1 Hold wall fronts and backs together in pairs, wrong sides facing. Referring to photo throughout, use light terra cotta yarn to Whipstitch bottom edges of wall fronts and backs to base; Whipstitch front and back together along remaining edges.

2 Using ivory yarn, Whipstitch four posts together along sides to form tall, square pillar; Overcast open ends with light terra cotta yarn. Hot-glue bottom of post and side to adjacent edge of sign.

3 Hot-glue wall caps atop walls, abutting posts.

4 Center and hot-glue post cap bottom to top of each post; center and hot-glue post cap top to post cap bottom.

5 Center and glue signs to front walls.

Finishing

1 Paint wooden balls ivory; let dry. Hot-glue ball atop each post.

2 Referring to photo, hot-glue pompoms to base around edges of walls to suggest bushes.

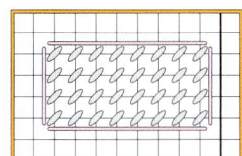

City Park Gates Wall
11 holes x 7 holes
Cut 4
Stitch 2 as shown for fronts;
stitch 2 completely in light terra cotta
Continental Stitches for backs

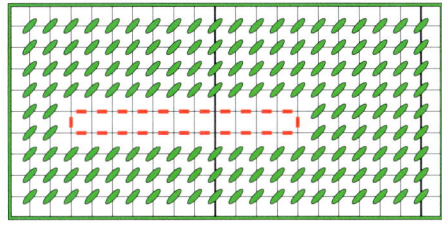

City Park Gates Base
21 holes x 10 holes
Cut 2; work as mirror images

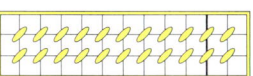

City Park Wall Cap
12 holes x 3 holes
Cut 2

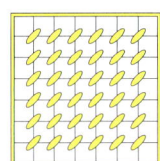

City Gates Post Cap Bottom
7 holes x 7 holes
Cut 2

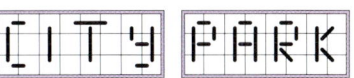

City Gates Signs
8 holes x 3 holes
Cut 1 each from 10-count plastic canvas

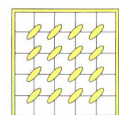

City Gates Post Cap Top
5 holes x 5 holes
Cut 2

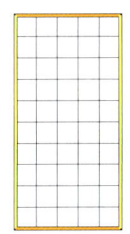

City Park Gates Post
5 holes x 10 holes
Cut 8

COLOR KEY	
Yards	**Worsted Weight Yarn**
14 (12.8m)	☐ Ivory
8 (7.3m)	■ Grass green
3 (2.7m)	☐ Light gray
20 (18.3m)	Uncoded areas are light terra cotta Continental Stitches
	∕ Light terra cotta Overcasting
	6-strand Embroidery Floss
10 (9.1m)	Uncoded areas on signs are ivory (12-strand) Continental Stitches
	∕ Ivory (12-strand) Overcasting
2 (1.8m)	∕ Ivory Straight Stitch
	∕ Black Backstitch and Straight Stitch

Park Fountain

Size: 3 inches diameter x 2¼ inches H
(7.6cm x 5.7cm)
Skill Level: Intermediate

Materials

- Plastic canvas:
  ⅙ sheet stiff 7-count
  Small amount flexible 7-count
  2 (3-inch) plastic canvas circles
- Worsted weight yarn as listed in color key
- Metallic cord as listed in color key
- Blue metallic chenille stem
- Pompoms
  13 (3mm) light green
  5 (5mm) green
  5 (¼-inch/0.6cm) green
- Size 18 tapestry needle
- Hot-glue gun and glue stick

Stitching Step by Step

1 From stiff plastic canvas, cut water and base according to graphs.

2 From flexible plastic canvas, cut fountain side according to graph.

3 Trim three outermost rows off both 3-inch plastic canvas circles. For fountain top, leave a ring one hole wide, and trim out remaining plastic canvas from center. Leave remaining piece as is for fountain bottom; it will remain unstitched.

4 Using grass green yarn, fill base with Continental Stitches; Overcast edges.

5 Using royal blue metallic craft cord, fill in water with Continental Stitches; Overcast all edges.

6 Bend strip for fountain side into a ring, overlapping ends by three holes each. Using light gray yarn, fill in strip with Continental Stitches, stitching through both layers on overlapped ends. Whipstitch bottom edge of fountain side to fountain bottom.

7 Cut chenille stem into three 4-inch (10.2cm) pieces. Hold pieces together, staggering ends so that each is 1/4 inch (0.6cm) from the next. Referring to photo throughout, bend the tops into hooks facing in different directions. Apply a small amount of hot glue inside stems to hold them together.

8 Insert bottom ends of chenille stems through opening in water. Push stems through plastic canvas until tallest piece extends 2 inches (5cm) above water.

9 Turn water over. Flatten ends of chenille stems against water as flat as possible, pointing them in different directions. Secure each end to wrong side of water with a small amount of hot glue.

10 Apply additional hot glue to wrong side of water; position water inside fountain and press down onto fountain bottom.

11 Slide fountain top over water spouts; using light gray yarn throughout, Whipstitch outer edge to top edge of fountain sides. Overcast inner edges.

Finishing

1 Center and hot-glue fountain on stitched base.

2 Referring to photo, hot-glue groups of three to five pompoms to base around fountain to suggest bushes.

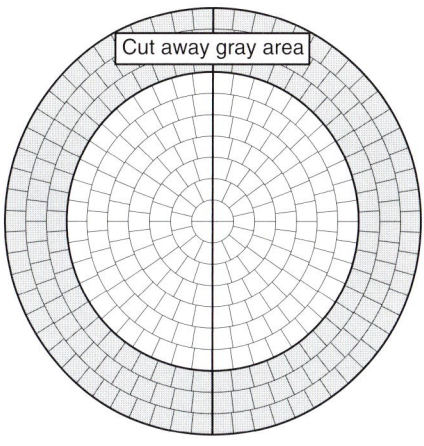

Fountain Bottom
Cut 1 from 3-inch plastic canvas circle;
it will remain unstitched

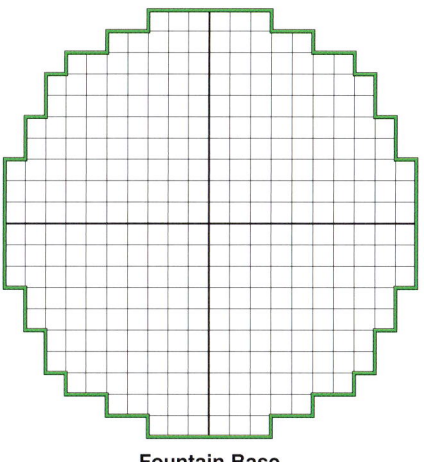

Fountain Base
20 holes x 20 holes
Cut 1

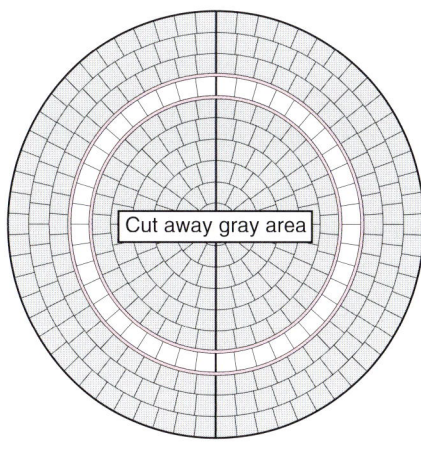

Fountain Top
Cut 1 from 3-inch plastic canvas circle

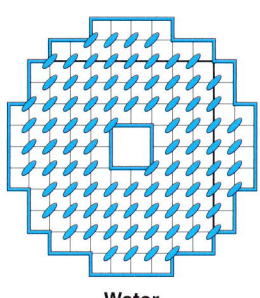

Water
12 holes x 12 holes
Cut 1

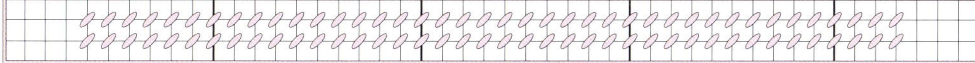

Fountain Sides
47 holes x 3 holes
Cut 1 from flexible 7-count plastic canvas

COLOR KEY	
Yards	**Worsted Weight Yarn**
8 (7.3m)	▢ Light gray
10 (9.1m)	Uncoded areas on fountain base are grass green Continental Stitches
	╱ Grass green Overcasting
	Metallic Craft Cord
4 (3.7m)	▢ Royal blue

The Needlecraft Shop • Berne, IN 46711 • NeedlecraftShop.com • *Main Street Village* 23

Victory Garden

Size: 2¼ inches W x 3¼ inches H x 2 inches D
(5.7cm x 8.2cm x 5cm)
Skill Level: Intermediate

Materials

- Plastic canvas:
  - Small amount stiff 7-count
  - Small amount white 7-count
  - Small amount clear 14-count
- Worsted weight yarn as listed in color key
- 6-strand cotton embroidery floss as listed in color key
- White sewing thread
- Tapestry needles: sizes #18 and #22
- Sharp sewing needle
- Hot-glue gun and glue stick

Stitching Step by Step

1 Cut garden base from stiff plastic canvas, sign from 14-count plastic canvas, and all fence pieces from white 7-count plastic canvas according to graphs; fences will remain unstitched.

2 Using dark brown yarn, fill in uncoded areas of garden base with Continental Stitches; work light gray Continental Stitches along front of garden. Leave red dashed lines unworked; these are Whipstitching lines, and will be stitched during assembly.

3 Add vegetables to garden rows using embroidery stitches:

Row 1—Using a double strand of dark kelly green yarn, work Turkey Loop Stitches to suggest radish tops; using red yarn, work Running Stitches next to green stitches to suggest radishes growing partially below ground.

Row 2—Using a double strand of lime green yarn, work large French Knots to suggest cabbages, wrapping floss around needle three times.

Row 3—Using medium kelly green yarn, work Turkey Loop Stitches to suggest carrot tops; clip loops and fluff cut ends with a needle. Using orange yarn, work Running Stitches down row next to green stitches to suggest carrots growing partially below ground.

Row 4—Using 12 strands leaf green floss, work pairs of Lazy Daisy Stitches with pointed ends facing. Using 12 strands very pale green floss, work French Knot in the center of each pair of Lazy Daisy Stitches.

4 Stitch sign according to graph, filling in uncoded area with white floss Continental Stitches; Overcast edges as you stitch.

5 Using 3 strands royal blue embroidery floss, Backstitch lettering on sign.

Assembly

1 Using camel yarn throughout, Whipstitch front fence along red dashed Whipstitching lines; Whipstitch side and back fences to side and back edges of garden base.

2 Using sewing needle and white thread, tack sign to sign area over entrance; secure with a few drops of hot glue.

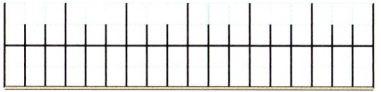

Victory Garden Left Side Fence
18 holes x 4 holes
Cut 1 from white plastic canvas;
cut away blue lines

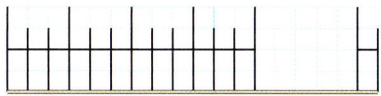

Victory Garden Right Side Fence
18 holes x 4 holes
Cut 1 from white plastic canvas;
cut away blue lines

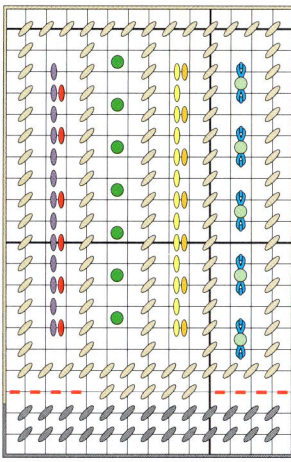

Victory Garden Base
14 holes x 21 holes
Cut 1

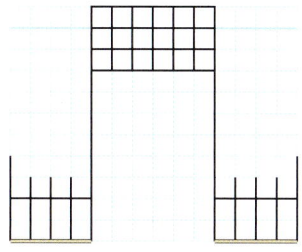

Victory Garden Front Fence
14 holes x 11 holes
Cut 1 from white plastic canvas;
cut away blue lines

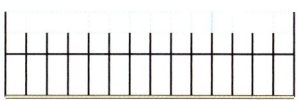

Victory Garden Back Fence
14 holes x 4 holes
Cut 1 from white plastic canvas;
cut away blue lines

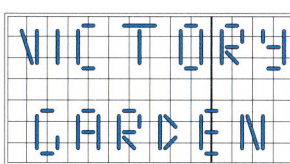

Victory Garden Sign
14 holes x 7 holes
Cut 1 from 14-count plastic canvas

Turkey Loop Stitch

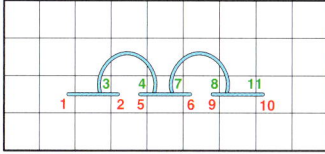

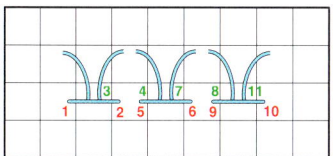

The top diagram shows this stitch left intact, as it is worked for the radish tops. The bottom graph demonstrates the cut Turkey Loop Stitch, as it is worked for the carrot tops. Because each stitch is anchored, cutting the loop will not cause the stitches to come out. A group of cut loop stitches gives a fluffy, soft look and feel to your project.

Running Stitch

COLOR KEY	
Yards	Worsted Weight Yarn
9 (8.2m)	☐ Camel
2 (1.8m)	■ Light gray
5 (4.6m)	Uncoded areas on garden base are dark brown Continental Stitches
3 (2.7m)	● Dark kelly green (2-strand) Turkey Loops
2 (1.8m)	● Medium kelly green Turkey Loops
1 (0.9m)	● Orange Running Stitch
1 (0.9m)	● Red Running Stitch
3 (2.7m)	● Lime green (2-strand) French Knot
	6-strand Embroidery Floss
3 (2.7m)	Uncoded areas on sign are white Continental Stitches
	╱ White Overcasting
3 (2.7m)	◁ Leaf green (12-strand) Lazy Daisy Stitch
1 (0.9m)	╱ Royal blue (3-strand) Backstitch
3 (2.7m)	● Very pale green (12-ply) French Knot

Market

Size: 4½ inches W x 2¾ inches H x 3 inches D
(11.4cm x 7cm x 7.6cm)
Skill Level: Advanced

Materials

- Plastic canvas:
    ½ sheet stiff 7-count
    Small amount clear 10-count
    Small amount clear 14-count
    3-inch radial circle
- Worsted weight yarn as listed in color key
- 6-strand cotton embroidery floss as listed in color key
- 4 (4mm) opaque white faceted beads
- 2 inches (5mm) green medium rickrack
- Tapestry needles: sizes #18 and #22
- Hot-glue gun and glue stick

Stitching Step by Step

1 From stiff plastic canvas, cut all walls, doorstep, awning support, base and roof pieces according to graphs.

2 From 10-count plastic canvas, cut window top and sides and produce bins according to graphs.

3 From 14-count plastic canvas, cut sign according to graph.

4 For awning, trim plastic canvas from 3-inch radial circle according to graph.

5 Stitch all walls, doorstep, roof and base pieces according to graphs, noting that much of the base will remain unstitched, and filling in uncoded areas with white Continental Stitches. Leave red dashed lines unworked; these are Whipstitching lines, and will be stitched during assembly. Overcast all edges of awning support with white yarn, window opening with light aqua yarn, doorstep with light terra cotta yarn, roof with kelly green yarn, and light gray areas of base with light gray yarn as you work Continental Stitches.

6 Fill in piece cut from radial circle with kelly green Continental Stitches for awning, Overcasting edges as you stitch. Wrap light spring green yarn around awning to form vertical stripes, securing each stripe on back of plastic canvas.

7 Using 6 strands embroidery floss, stitch sign according to graph, Overcasting edges with white floss as you stitch sign.

8 Using 12 strands embroidery floss throughout, stitch market window top and sides according to graphs using light aqua floss, reversing one side before stitching. Work kelly green Continental Stitches on produce bins.

9 Add embroidery stitches using yarn as follows: gold—Straight Stitch door handles; light spring green—Straight Stitch along top of front wall and edges of sign on left-side wall; cornflower blue—Straight Stitch border on left side wall and windowsills on back wall; dark green—Straight Stitch bushes.

10 Add embroidery stitches using floss as follows: black—Straight Stitch around doors and lettering on left side wall; black (3-ply)—Backstitch lettering on market sign; lime green—Overcast apple stems on market sign; kelly green—Straight Stitch around window in front wall and around sides and tops of windows on back wall.

11 Add remaining embroidery stitches to produce bins. *Note: Fill the squares loosely; the green background stitching should show around each square. Random stitches are fine; don't be concerned about covering every bit of plastic canvas with stitching.*

- Limes (square 1)—lime green floss French Knots, worked in five rows of five, and staggering positions of knots.
- Cabbages (square 2)—Light spring green yarn French Knots, worked in three evenly spaced rows of three knots each. If the yarn is too thick to pass through the holes, use only 3 plies yarn.
- Cauliflowers (square 3)—French Knots stitched with 12 strands off-white floss, worked in four rows of four French Knots each.
- Lemons (square 4)—Yellow floss French Knots worked in two rows of three, then two rows of two.
- Carrots (square 5)—Orange yarn vertical Straight Stitches, worked in two rows, with one less stitch at end of top row.
- Apples (square 6)—Red floss French Knots worked in four rows of three knots each.
- Grapes (square 7)—Purple floss French Knots, worked in one row of four, two rows of three, and then one row of four.

Assembly

1 Using 12 strands light aqua floss throughout, Whipstitch long vertical edges of window sides to sides of produce bins, with right side of stitching facing in toward bins. Whipstitch window top to top edges of window sides and produce bins; Overcast remaining edges.

2 Using white yarn, Whipstitch bottom edge of front wall to base. Position display window behind opening in wall so that bottom of edge of produce bins rests snugly in corner between front wall and base; hot-glue display window with produce bins in place.

3 Using dark green yarn, Whipstitch bottom edges of left and right side walls to base along Whipstitching lines; Whipstitch bottom edge of back wall to edge of base. Overcast remaining unfinished edges of base.

4 Using white yarn throughout, Whipstitch walls together at corners; Overcast top edges of walls.

Finishing

1 Hot-glue one long edge of awning support above window as shown. Hot-glue rickrack along front edge to suggest rolled-up awning.

2 Hot-glue front door awning above door.

3 Center and hot-glue market sign in area of green stitching above window.

4 Hot-glue doorstep to base in front of front door.

5 Center and hot-glue roof to top of market.

6 Thread beads onto extensions along top of front wall as shown; secure with tiny drops of glue.

7 Cut four "trees" ranging in height from ½ inch (1.3cm) to 1½ inches (3.8cm) from bumpy chenille, with tapered ends of bumps as treetops. Hot-glue trees to base as shown.

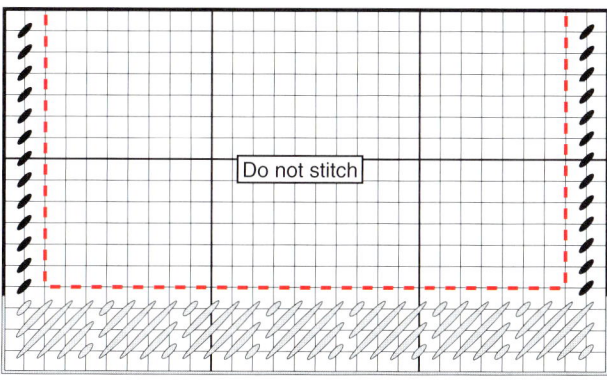

Market Base
29 holes x 17 holes
Cut 1

COLOR KEY	
Yards	Worsted Weight Yarn
16 (14.6m)	Kelly green
8 (7.3m)	Dark green
5 (4.6m)	Light aqua
4 (3.7m)	Light gray
4 (3.7m)	Light spring green
3 (2.7m)	Cornflower blue
1 (0.9m)	Light terra cotta
15 (13.7m)	Uncoded areas on walls are white Continental Stitch
1 (0.9m)	Orange Straight Stitch
	White Overcasting
1 (0.9m)	Gold Straight Stitch
	Dark green Straight Stitch
	Light spring green Straight Stitch
	Cornflower blue Straight Stitch
	Light spring green French Knot
	6-strand Embroidery Floss
20 (18.3m)	Light aqua (12-strand)
12 (11m)	Kelly green (12-strand)
4 (3.7m)	Black (3-strand) Backstitch
	Black (6-strand) Backstitch and Straight Stitch
	Kelly green Straight Stitch
3 (2.7m)	Off-white (12-strand) French Knot
2 (1.8m)	Red (12-strand)
3 (2.7m)	Uncoded areas on sign are white Continental Stitches
	White Overcasting
2 (1.8m)	Lime green French Knot
	Lime green Overcasting
1 (0.9m)	Yellow French Knot
1 (0.9m)	Purple French Knot
	Red French Knot

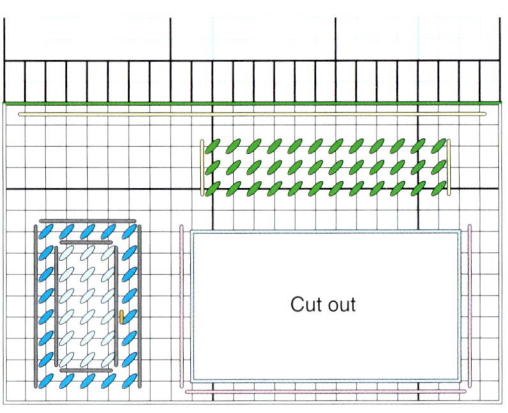

Market Front Wall
24 holes x 18 holes
Cut 1,
cut away blue lines

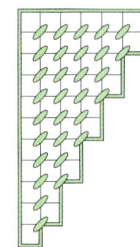

Market Window Side
6 holes x 11 holes
Cut 2 from 10-count plastic canvas;
reverse 1 before stitching

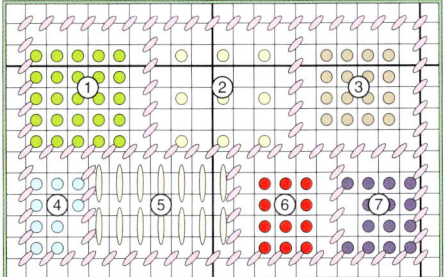

Market Produce Bins
21 holes x 13 holes
Cut 1 from 10-count plastic canvas

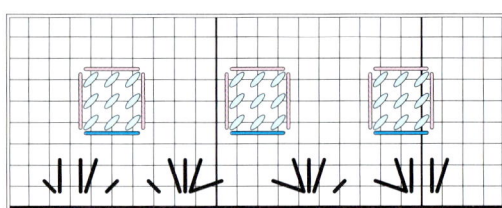

Market Back Wall
24 holes x 9 holes
Cut 1

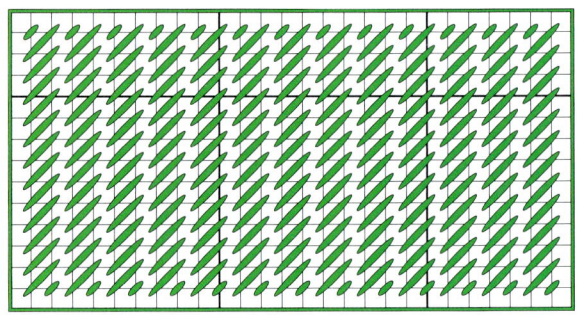

Market Roof
27 holes x 14 holes
Cut 1

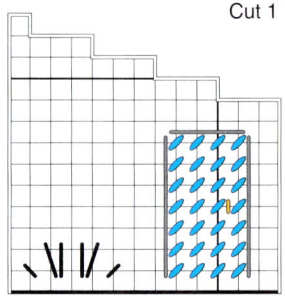

Market Right Side Wall
13 holes x 13 holes
Cut 1

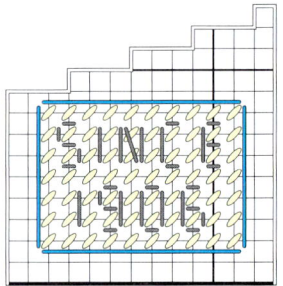

Market Left Side Wall
13 holes x 13 holes
Cut 1

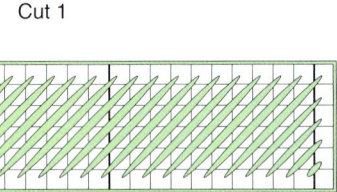

Market Window Top
21 holes x 6 holes
Cut 1 from 10-count plastic canvas

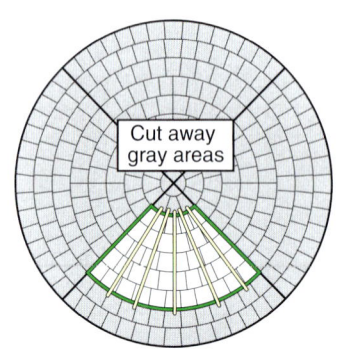

Market Awning
Cut 1 from 3-inch plastic canvas circle

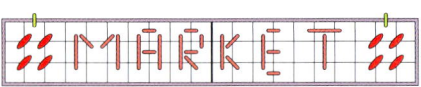

Market Sign
20 holes x 3 holes
Cut 1 from 14-count plastic canvas

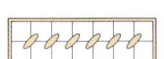

Market Doorstep
7 holes x 2 holes
Cut 1

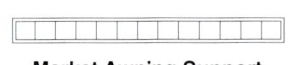

Market Awning Support
13 holes x 1 holes
Cut 1

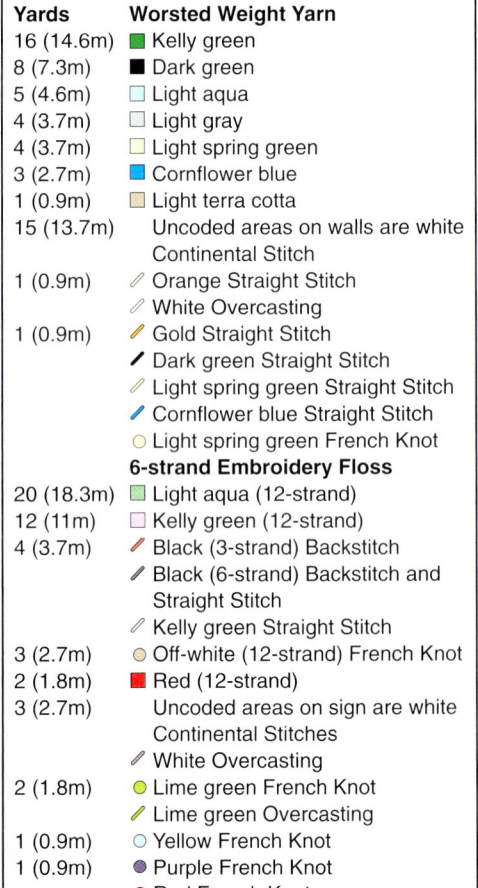

COLOR KEY

Yards	Worsted Weight Yarn
16 (14.6m)	■ Kelly green
8 (7.3m)	■ Dark green
5 (4.6m)	□ Light aqua
4 (3.7m)	□ Light gray
4 (3.7m)	□ Light spring green
3 (2.7m)	■ Cornflower blue
1 (0.9m)	□ Light terra cotta
15 (13.7m)	Uncoded areas on walls are white Continental Stitch
1 (0.9m)	∕ Orange Straight Stitch
	∕ White Overcasting
1 (0.9m)	∕ Gold Straight Stitch
	∕ Dark green Straight Stitch
	∕ Light spring green Straight Stitch
	∕ Cornflower blue Straight Stitch
	○ Light spring green French Knot

6-strand Embroidery Floss

20 (18.3m)	■ Light aqua (12-strand)
12 (11m)	■ Kelly green (12-strand)
4 (3.7m)	∕ Black (3-strand) Backstitch
	∕ Black (6-strand) Backstitch and Straight Stitch
	∕ Kelly green Straight Stitch
3 (2.7m)	○ Off-white (12-strand) French Knot
2 (1.8m)	■ Red (12-strand)
3 (2.7m)	Uncoded areas on sign are white Continental Stitches
	∕ White Overcasting
2 (1.8m)	● Lime green French Knot
	∕ Lime green Overcasting
1 (0.9m)	○ Yellow French Knot
1 (0.9m)	● Purple French Knot
	● Red French Knot

Firehouse

Size: 5 inches W x 6½ inches H x 4 inches D
(12.7cm x 16.5cm x 10.2cm)
Skill Level: Advanced

Materials

❏ Plastic canvas:
   1½ sheets stiff 7-count
   Small amount clear 10-count
   Small amount clear 14-count
❏ Worsted weight yarn as listed in color key
❏ 6-strand cotton embroidery floss as listed in color key
❏ Clear faceted beads:
   3 (6mm)
   2 (4mm)
❏ Metallic silver melon beads:
   1 (14mm)
   1 (10mm)
❏ 3 (8mm) metallic silver bell caps
❏ Sewing thread:
   Black
   Gray
   White
❏ Tapestry needles: sizes #18 and #22
❏ Sharp sewing needle
❏ Hot-glue gun and glue stick

Stitching Step by Step

Firehouse

1 From stiff plastic canvas, cut all firehouse walls, garage door, both firehouse roof pieces, both steps and firehouse facade caps A–C according to graphs.

2 Stitch walls according to graphs, filling in uncoded areas with dark red Continental Stitches. Leave red dashed lines unworked; these are Whipstitching lines, and will be stitched during assembly. Overcast garage door opening using dark red yarn.

3 Stitch garage door, roof and steps according to graphs, leaving one corner of roof unstitched as shown, and Overcasting edges with matching colors as you stitch.

4 Using off-white yarn throughout, stitch facade caps according to graphs. Whipstitch facade caps B together along one short end; Overcast all remaining edges on all facade cap pieces.

5 Add embroidery stitches using full strands of yarn as follows: off-white—Straight Stitch sides and tops of small doors on front and side walls; Straight Stitch tops of rectangular windows on walls; Straight Stitch square around octagonal windows and Backstitch details on lower cupola; gold—French Knot doorknobs on smaller doors on front and side walls.

6 Using 1 ply separated from a length of off-white yarn, Straight Stitch around window on garage door.

7 Add embroidery stitches using cotton embroidery floss as follows: 6 strands black—Backstitch and Straight Stitch around octagonal windows, and down sides, across bottoms and across panes of rectangular windows; 12 strands lime green—Lazy Daisy Stitches along bottoms of walls.

Signs & Cupola

1 From 14-count plastic canvas, cut firehouse sign according to graph.

2 From 10-count plastic canvas, cut firehouse year plaque according to graphs.

3 From stiff plastic canvas, cut all cupola walls and cupola roof pieces according to graphs.

4 Using 6 strands black embroidery floss throughout, stitch sign according to graph, filling in uncoded areas with Continental Stitches; Overcast edges as you stitch.

5 Using 12 strands off-white embroidery floss throughout, fill in uncoded areas of year plaque with Continental Stitches; Overcast edges as you stitch.

6 Stitch cupola wall and roof pieces according to graphs, filling in uncoded areas on upper and lower cupola walls with dark red Continental Stitches; filling uncoded areas on cupola upper and lower roof pieces with off-white Continental Stitches; Overcast lower roof with off-white yarn as you stitch.

7 Using a full strand of off-white yarn, Straight Stitch top points and down center of black siren grates on upper cupola front and back; Straight Stitch square around octagonal windows and Backstitch details on lower cupola walls.

8 Using 1 ply separated from a length of off-white yarn, work horizontal Straight Stitches across black siren grates on upper cupola front and back.

9 Add embroidery stitches using embroidery floss as follows: 6 strands black—Backstitch and Straight Stitch around light aqua windows on lower cupola sides and upper cupola front and back, and Backstitch year on year plaque; 3 strands gold—Backstitch lettering on sign and add French Knot.

Firehouse Addition & Base

1 From stiff plastic canvas, cut firehouse addition main wall and side walls, addition roof, and base pieces according to graphs; base will remain unstitched.

2 Stitch addition roof and walls according to graphs, reversing one side wall before stitching and filling in uncoded areas with dark red Continental Stitches.

3 Using off-white yarn, Straight Stitch across tops of windows on side walls.

4 Add embroidery stitches using cotton embroidery floss as follows: 6 strands black—Straight Stitch around windows on main wall; Straight Stitch down sides and across bottoms of windows on side walls; 12 strands lime green—Lazy Daisy Stitches along bottoms of walls.

Assembly

1 Using sewing needle and black thread, tack garage door behind opening in firehouse wall.

2 Thread sewing needle with doubled gray sewing thread. Bring needle through front wall above smaller door, at lower red dot. Thread 6mm bead and bell cap onto thread so that cap fits on top of bead; take needle back through wall at upper red dot. Secure thread ends on back, using just enough tension to suspend "light" over door as shown. Repeat to add lights over doors on side walls.

3 Using off-white yarn throughout, Whipstitch addition main wall to shorter (front) edges of addition side walls; Overcast top edges. Overcast longer (back) edges of side walls to firehouse left side wall. Overcast bottom and side edges of addition roof; Whipstitch top edge to firehouse left side wall.

4 Using gray yarn, Whipstitch bottom edges of lower cupola walls to firehouse main roof according to graph. Using off-white yarn throughout, Whipstitch these lower cupola walls together along corner.

5 Bring sharp sewing needle threaded with doubled gray sewing thread through firehouse roof at red dot. Thread on 14mm melon bead, then 4mm bead; take needle back down through melon bead and same hole in roof. Bring needle back up through roof at blue dot; thread on 10mm melon bead and 4mm bead; take needle back down through melon bead and same hole in roof; secure thread ends on back.

6 Using grass green yarn throughout, Whipstitch bottom edges of firehouse walls and addition to edges of base, Overcasting base edge across garage door.

7 Fold up firehouse walls perpendicular to base. Using off-white yarn throughout, Whipstitch walls together along back two corners, then front left corner. Beginning at bottom, Whipstitch walls together along front right corner.

8 Position main roof inside the firehouse walls, one row below the top edges of walls. Align lower cupola walls on roof with matching walls on firehouse front and right side walls; using off-white yarn, Whipstitch lower cupola together along remaining three corners.

9 Using dark red yarn, Overcast top edges of lower cupola; using off-white yarn, Overcast all remaining edges of firehouse.

10 Using sewing needle and white thread, loosely tack roof to firehouse walls, working through rows of off-white Continental Stitches just below top edges.

11 Using off-white yarn throughout, Whipstitch walls of upper cupola together to form an open cube; Overcast top and bottom edges.

12 Whipstitch cupola upper roof ends to upper roof sides; Whipstitch sides to upper roof center. Overcast remaining edges. Hot-glue upper roof over upper cupola as shown, bending up roof ends.

13 Hot-glue upper cupola in center of cupola lower roof; center and hot-glue lower roof to lower cupola.

14 Hot-glue joined facade caps B over peak of front firehouse wall, centering facade caps over edge of wall. Hot-glue facade cap A over edge of wall to left of peak; hot-glue facade cap C over edge of wall between peak and cupola.

15 Hot-glue underside of firehouse addition roof to top edges of addition walls. Hot-glue sign and year plaque to firehouse front wall as shown. Stack light gray steps; hot-glue outside door on right side wall.

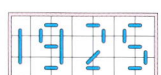
Firehouse Year Plaque
7 holes x 3 holes
Cut 1 from 10-count plastic canvas

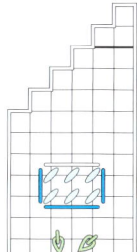
Firehouse Addition Side Wall
6 holes x 12 holes
Cut 2; reverse 1 before stitching

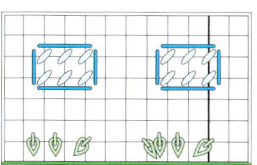
Firehouse Addition Main Wall
12 holes x 7 holes
Cut 1

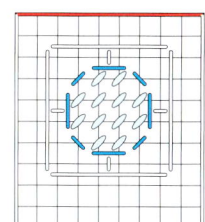
Firehouse Lower Cupola
9 holes x 10 holes
Cut 2

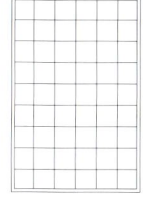
Firehouse Cupola Upper Roof Side
6 holes x 9 holes
Cut 2

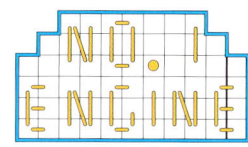
Firehouse Sign
11 holes x 6 holes
Cut 1 from 14-count plastic canvas

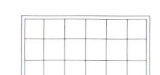
Firehouse Facade Cap B
6 holes x 3 holes
Cut 2

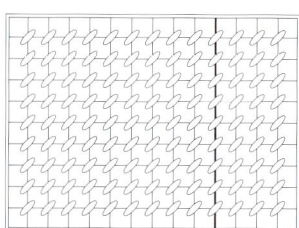
Firehouse Addition Roof
14 holes x 10 holes
Cut 1

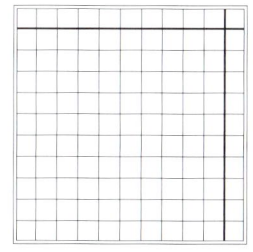
Firehouse Cupola Lower Roof
11 holes x 11 holes
Cut 1

COLOR KEY	
Yards	**Worsted Weight Yarn**
28 (25.6m)	☐ Off-white
14 (12.8m)	■ Gray
10 (9.1m)	■ Black
12 (11m)	☐ Light aqua
4 (3.7m)	■ Grass green
2 (1.8m)	☐ Light gray
45 (41.1m)	Uncoded areas on walls, addition and cupola are Dark red Continental Stitches
	Uncoded areas on facade caps and cupola lower roof are Off-white Continental Stitches
	╱ Dark red Overcasting
	╱ Off-white Backstitch and Straight Stitch
	╱ Off-white (1-ply) Straight Stitch
	6-strand Embroidery Floss
15 (13.7m)	Uncoded area on sign is Black Continental Stitches
10 (9.1m)	⬬ Lime green (12-strand) Lazy Daisy
4 (3.7m)	Uncoded areas of year plaque are Off-white (12-strand) Continental Stitches
	╱ Off-white (12-strand) Overcasting
1 (0.9m)	╱ Gold (3-strand) Backstitch
	● Gold (3-strand) French Knot
	╱ Black Backstitch and Straight Stitch

*The Needlecraft Shop • Berne, IN 46711 • NeedlecraftShop.com • **Main Street Village 31***

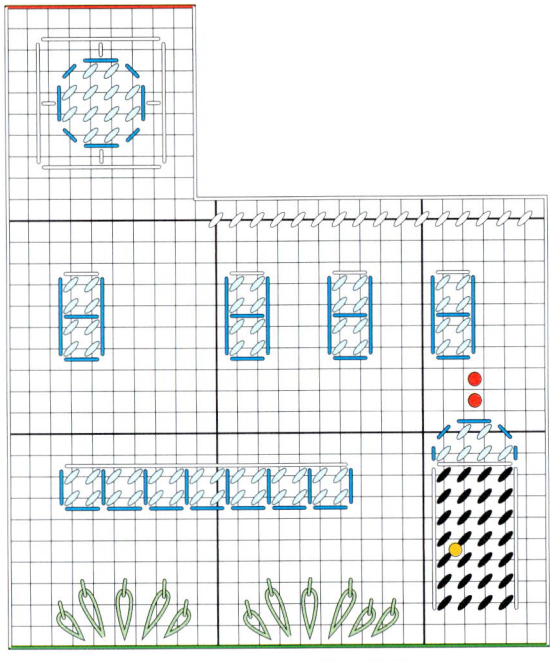

Firehouse Right Side Wall
26 holes x 30 holes
Cut 1

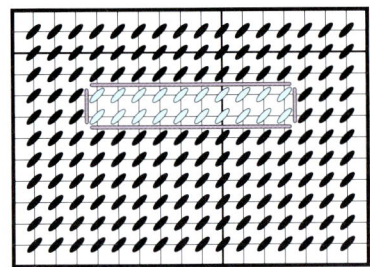

Firehouse Garage Door
17 holes x 12 holes
Cut 1

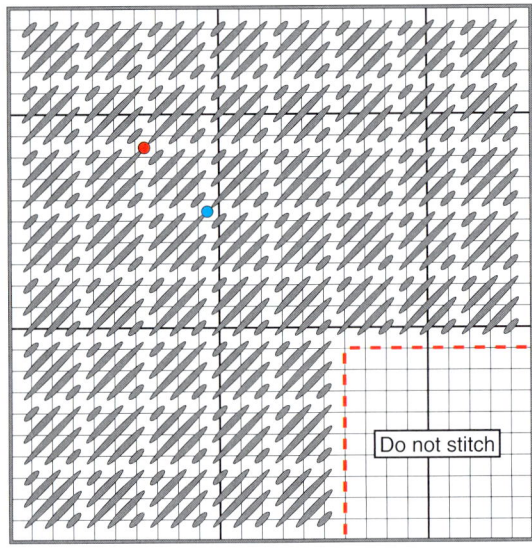

Firehouse Main Roof
25 holes x 25 holes
Cut 1

Firehouse Middle Step
4 holes x 3 holes
Cut 1

Firehouse Top Step
4 holes x 2 holes
Cut 1

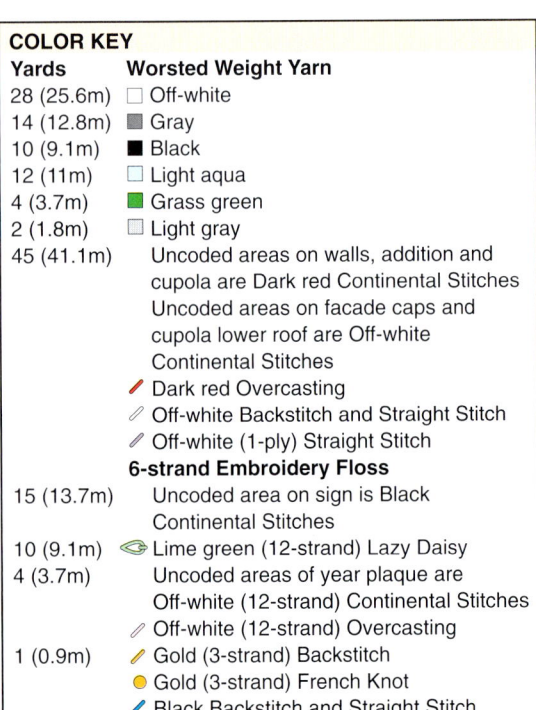

COLOR KEY

Yards	Worsted Weight Yarn
28 (25.6m)	☐ Off-white
14 (12.8m)	▦ Gray
10 (9.1m)	■ Black
12 (11m)	☐ Light aqua
4 (3.7m)	■ Grass green
2 (1.8m)	☐ Light gray
45 (41.1m)	Uncoded areas on walls, addition and cupola are Dark red Continental Stitches Uncoded areas on facade caps and cupola lower roof are Off-white Continental Stitches
	╱ Dark red Overcasting
	╱ Off-white Backstitch and Straight Stitch
	╱ Off-white (1-ply) Straight Stitch

6-strand Embroidery Floss

15 (13.7m)	Uncoded area on sign is Black Continental Stitches
10 (9.1m)	⬮ Lime green (12-strand) Lazy Daisy
4 (3.7m)	Uncoded areas of year plaque are Off-white (12-strand) Continental Stitches
	╱ Off-white (12-strand) Overcasting
1 (0.9m)	╱ Gold (3-strand) Backstitch
	● Gold (3-strand) French Knot
	╱ Black Backstitch and Straight Stitch

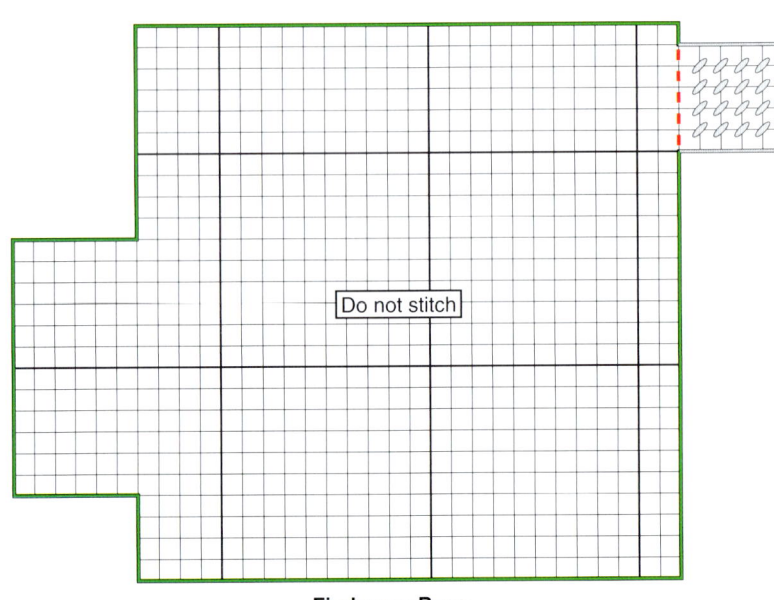

Firehouse Base
37 holes x 26 holes
Cut 1

32 *Main Street Village* • The Needlecraft Shop • Berne, IN 46711 • NeedlecraftShop.com

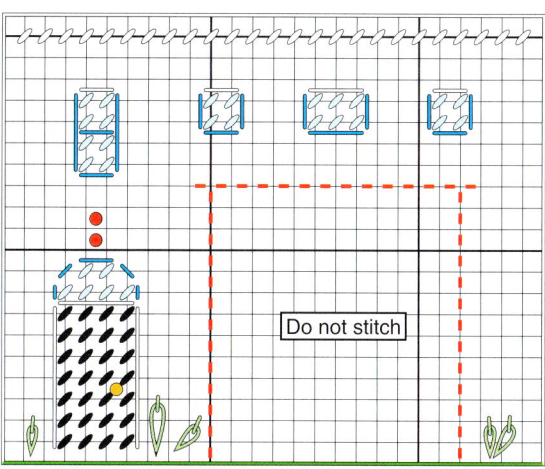

Firehouse Left Side Wall
26 holes x 21 holes
Cut 1

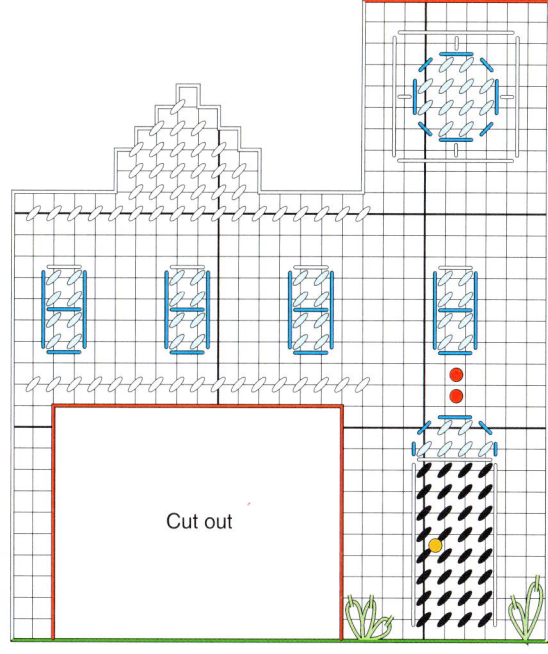

Firehouse Front Wall
26 holes x 30 holes
Cut 1

Firehouse Back Wall
26 holes x 21 holes
Cut 1

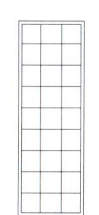

Firehouse Cupola Upper Roof Center
3 holes x 9 holes
Cut 1

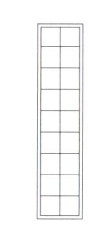

Firehouse Cupola Upper Roof End
2 holes x 9 holes
Cut 2

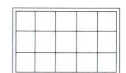

Firehouse Facade Cap A
5 holes x 3 holes
Cut 2

Firehouse Facade Cap C
4 holes x 3 holes
Cut 1

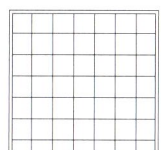

Firehouse Upper Cupola Sides
7 holes x 7 holes
Cut 2

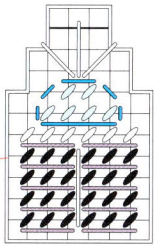

Firehouse Upper Cupola Front/Back
7 holes x 11 holes
Cut 2

The Needlecraft Shop • Berne, IN 46711 • NeedlecraftShop.com • **Main Street Village 33**

Quilt Shop

Size: 5 inches W x 4½ inches H x 3⅜ inches D
(12.7cm x 11.4cm x 8.6cm)
Skill Level: Advanced

Materials

- Plastic canvas:
    1 sheet stiff 7-count
    Small amount black 7-count
    Small amount white 7-count
    Small amount clear 10-count
- Worsted weight yarn as listed in color key
- 6-strand cotton embroidery floss as listed in color key
- White Venice lace trim:
    3 (⅜-inch/1cm x ¼-inch/0.6cm) scalloped motifs
    2 (1-inch/2.5cm x ¼-inch/0.6cm) motifs
- 4mm pearl beads-on-a-string:
    2 (6-inch) pieces
    1 (3-inch) piece
- Tiny silver bell
- Sewing thread:
    White
    Black
- Tapestry needles: #18 and #22
- Sewing needle
- Hot-glue gun and glue stick

Stitching Step by Step

1 From stiff plastic canvas, cut all walls, including cantilever pieces, roof pieces, shutters and base according to graphs; base will remain unstitched.

2 From black plastic canvas, cut one bell bracket according to graph; it will remain unstitched.

3 From white plastic canvas, cut one window and both roof railings according to graphs; they will remain unstitched.

4 From 10-count plastic canvas, cut one quilt shop sign according to graph.

5 Stitch all walls, cantilever pieces and roof pieces according to graphs, filling in uncoded areas on walls and cantilever side and bottom with white Continental Stitches. Leave red dashed lines unworked; these are Whipstitching lines, and will be stitched during assembly.

6 Add embroidery stitches with yarn as follows, using a full strand of yarn unless instructed otherwise: dark periwinkle (1-ply)—Straight Stitch around doors; black—Straight Stitch door hinges and handles; lavender—Straight Stitch decorations on walls at tops of gables; periwinkle (1-ply)—Straight Stitch windowpanes in round windows; lime green—Straight Stitch bushes around house.

7 Add embroidery stitches using 6-strand cotton embroidery floss as follows: lavender—Straight Stitch around all aqua windows; red-orange—French Knot flowers in bushes.

8 Stitch shutters, Overcasting top, bottom and one side of each with dark periwinkle; Whipstitch shutters to windows along remaining side edges.

9 Using 12 strands white floss throughout, stitch quilt sign according to graph, filling in uncoded area with Continental Stitches and Overcasting edges as you stitch. Using 6 strands black floss, Straight Stitch lettering on sign.

Assembly

1 Using white yarn throughout, Whipstitch one long edge of cantilever bottom to front wall along bottom of window, and long edge of cantilever side to front wall along right edge of window where indicated. Using periwinkle yarn, Whipstitch cantilever top along top of window.

2 Using lime green yarn, Whipstitch front wall and cantilever wall to base along front edge (B) and left side edge (A) respectively.

3 With cantilever wall (left side wall) facing you, use white yarn to Whipstitch front and cantilever walls together along corner, working straight up through the protrusion on the cantilever wall to join walls with Continental Stitch.

4 Using white yarn throughout, Whipstitch window to adjacent edges of cantilever sides and bottom; Whipstitch cantilever sides and bottom together along adjacent edges. Using periwinkle yarn throughout, Whipstitch top edge of window to front edge of cantilever top pieces; Whipstitch adjacent edges of cantilever top and sides.

5 Using lime green yarn, Whipstitch all remaining walls to base.

6 Using white yarn throughout, Whipstitch extension side walls to quilt shop inside wall where indicated. Whipstitch walls together along all remaining pieces.

7 Overcast top edges of walls.

8 With right side of roof stitching facing out, sandwich shorter roof railing between matching edges of gable roof, matching top row of holes in railing with top row of holes in roof pieces. Using periwinkle yarn throughout, Whipstitch through all layers; Overcast remaining edges.

9 In the same manner, stitch longer railing between matching edges of inside and outside roof; Overcast edges.

10 Using black thread and sharp sewing needle, tack long edge of bell bracket to front wall over door.

11 Using white thread and sharp sewing needle, tack lengths of iridescent beads along outer top edges of gable walls, attaching the 6-inch pieces to the font and back walls and the 3-inch piece to the extension wall. Trim excess beads as needed.

12 Position main roof over quilt shop's front and back walls, centering it so that cutout on edge of inside roof faces the extension. Hot-glue roof to quilt shop.

13 Position gable roof on top of extensions with lower edges of inside of roof matching lower edges of main roof. The peak of the roof should abut the main roof snugly. Hot-glue gable roof in place.

Finishing

1 Hot-glue ⅜-inch (1cm) lace motifs to tops of gables as shown to suggest decorative trusses. Hot-glue 1-inch (2.5cm) lace motifs above round windows as shown.

2 Using black thread and sharp sewing needle, sew bell to bottom horizontal edge of bell bracket, making a tiny loop between the bell's metal hanging loop and the bracket. Knot and trim so that bell hangs above the door.

3 Hot-glue sign to front wall as shown.

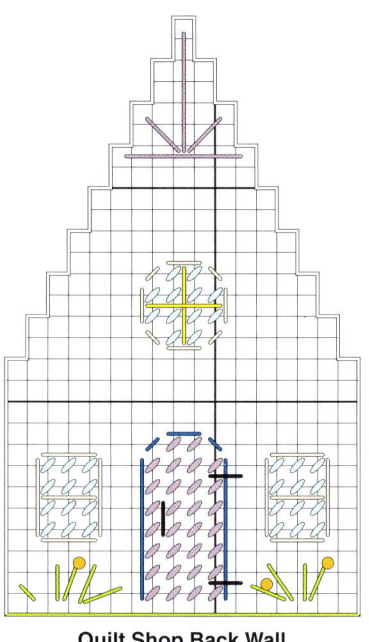

Quilt Shop Back Wall
17 holes x 28 holes
Cut 1

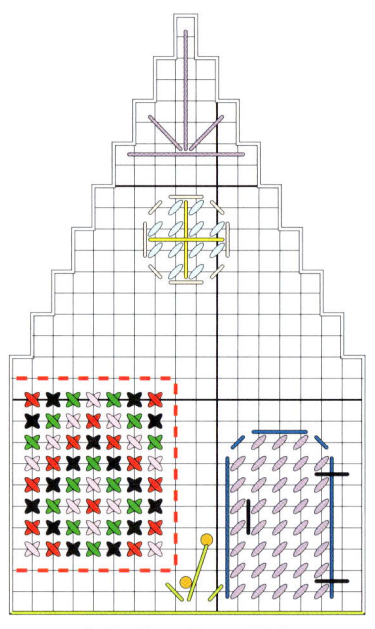

Quilt Shop Front Wall
17 holes x 28 holes
Cut 1

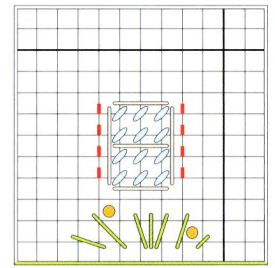

Quilt Shop Extension Side Wall
12 holes x 12 holes
Cut 2

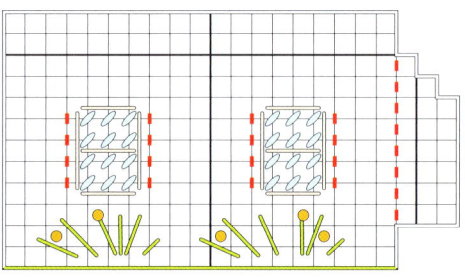

Quilt Shop Cantilever Wall
22 holes x 12 holes
Cut 1

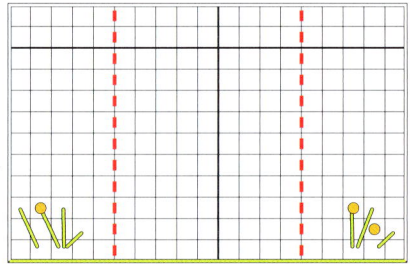

Quilt Shop Inside Wall
19 holes x 12 holes
Cut 1

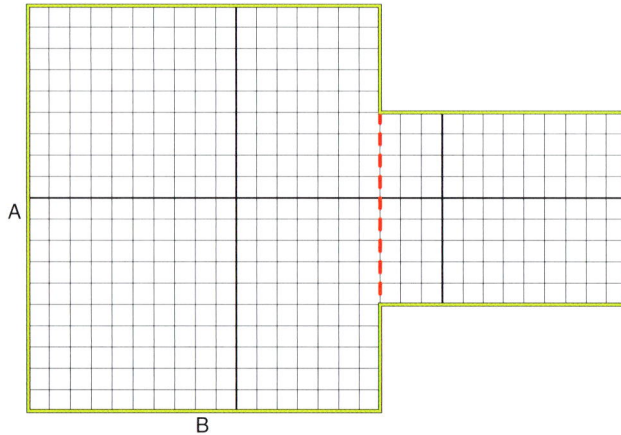

Quilt Shop Base
29 holes x 19 holes
Cut 1;
it will remain unstitched

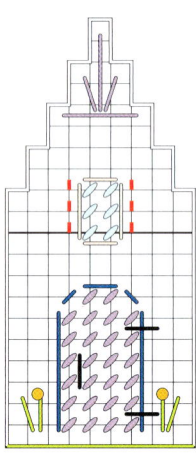

Quilt Shop Extension End Wall
9 holes x 20 holes
Cut 1

36 *Main Street Village* • *The Needlecraft Shop* • *Berne, IN 46711* • *NeedlecraftShop.com*

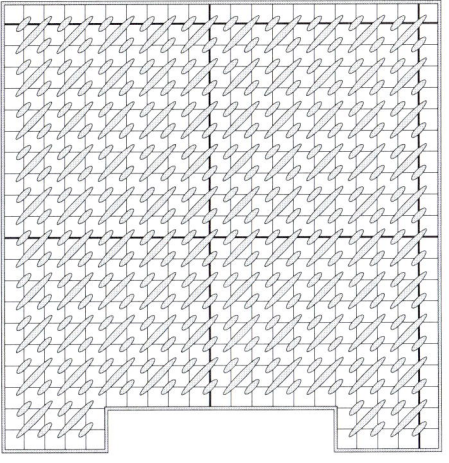

Quilt Shop Inside Roof
21 holes x 21 holes
Cut 1

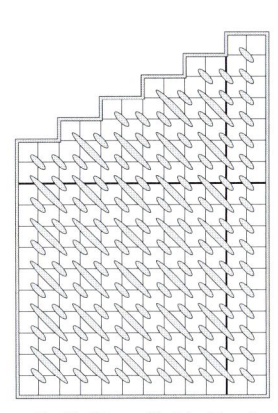

Quilt Shop Gable Roof
12 holes x 17 holes
Cut 2; reverse 1 before stitching

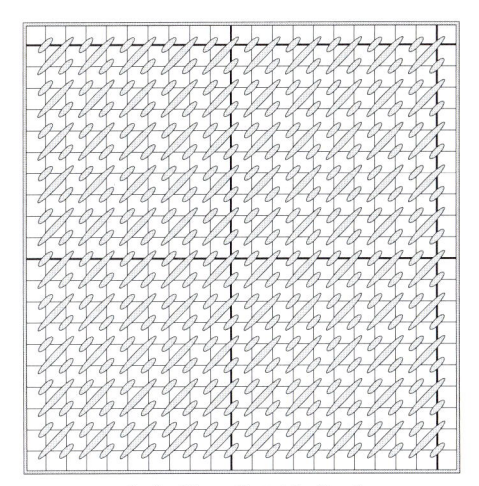

Quilt Shop Outside Roof
21 holes x 21 holes
Cut 1

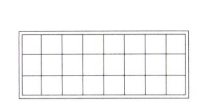

Quilt Shop Cantilever Bottom
8 holes x 3 holes
Cut 1

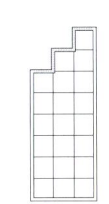

Quilt Shop Cantilever Side
8 holes x 3 holes
Cut 1

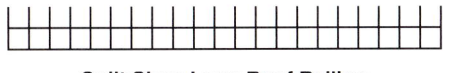

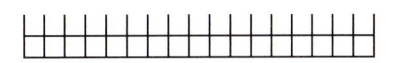

Quilt Shop Long Roof Railing
21 holes x 2 holes
Cut 1 from white plastic canvas;
it will remain unstitched

Quilt Shop Short Roof Railing
17 holes x 2 holes
Cut 1 from white plastic canvas;
it will remain unstitched

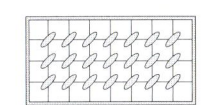

Quilt Shop Cantilever Top
8 holes x 4 holes
Cut 1

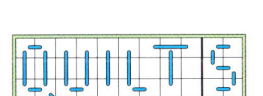

Quilt Shop Sign
11 holes x 3 holes
Cut 1 from 10-count plastic canvas

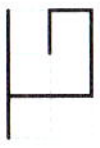

Quilt Shop Bell Bracket
2 holes x 3 holes
Cut 1 from black plastic canvas;
it will remain unstitched,
cut away blue lines

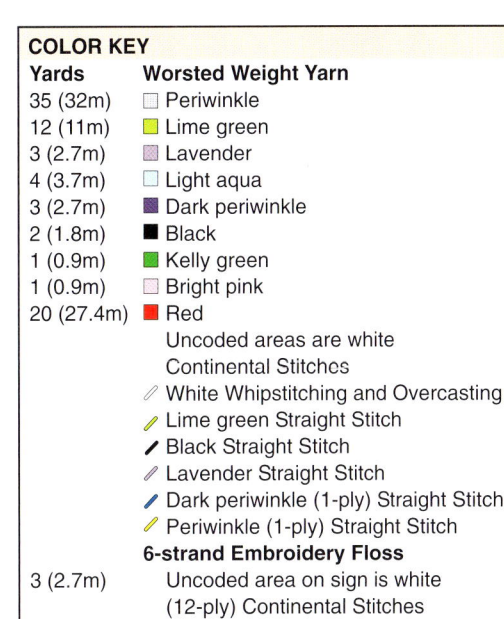

Quilt Shop Narrow Shutter
1 hole x 3 holes
Cut 2

Quilt Shop Window
8 holes x 6 holes
Cut 1 from white plastic canvas,
cut away blue lines

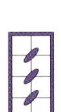

Quilt Shop Wide Shutter
2 holes x 4 holes
Cut 8

COLOR KEY

Yards	Worsted Weight Yarn
35 (32m)	Periwinkle
12 (11m)	Lime green
3 (2.7m)	Lavender
4 (3.7m)	Light aqua
3 (2.7m)	Dark periwinkle
2 (1.8m)	Black
1 (0.9m)	Kelly green
1 (0.9m)	Bright pink
20 (27.4m)	Red
	Uncoded areas are white Continental Stitches
	White Whipstitching and Overcasting
	Lime green Straight Stitch
	Black Straight Stitch
	Lavender Straight Stitch
	Dark periwinkle (1-ply) Straight Stitch
	Periwinkle (1-ply) Straight Stitch

6-strand Embroidery Floss

3 (2.7m)	Uncoded area on sign is white (12-ply) Continental Stitches
	White (12-ply) Overcasting
4 (3.7m)	Lavender Straight Stitch
2 (1.8m)	Black Backstitch and Straight Stitch
1 (0.9m)	Red-orange French Knot

Hanging Quilt

Size: 2½ inches W x 2¼ inches H x 1 inch D
(6.4cm x 5.7cm x 2.5cm)
Skill Level: Intermediate

Materials

- Plastic canvas:
    - Small amount stiff 7-count
    - Small amount white 7-count
    - Small amount clear 10-count
- Worsted weight yarn as listed in color key
- 6-strand cotton embroidery floss as listed in color key
- 2 (4mm) white pearl beads
- Tapestry needles: sizes #18 and #22
- Hot-glue gun and glue stick

Stitching Step by Step

1 Cut base from stiff plastic canvas, quilt from 10-count plastic canvas, and quilt support from white 7-count plastic canvas according to graphs; quilt support will remain unstitched.

2 Using lime green yarn throughout, fill in uncoded base with Continental Stitches, leaving red dashed lines unworked; these are Whipstitching lines and will be stitched during assembly. Overcast edges.

3 Stitch quilt according to graph. Using 12 strands black embroidery floss, Overcast edges according to graph, leaving hanging tabs unstitched.

Assembly

1 Using lime green yarn, Whipstitch bottom edge of quilt support to base.

2 Secure brown embroidery floss at back of quilt near one hanger hole. Bring floss through hanger hole; loop it over top of support. Keeping loop fairly loose, secure floss on back of quilt. Repeat to make second hanger at other hanger hole.

3 Hot-glue pearl bead over each vertical post on quilt support.

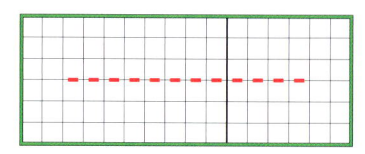

Hanging Quilt Base
16 holes x 6 holes
Cut 1

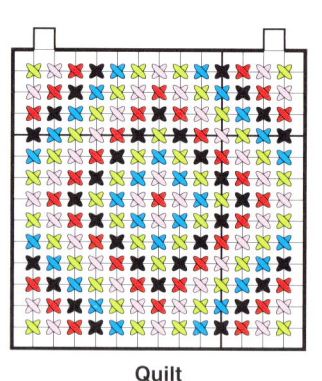

Quilt
14 holes x 15 holes
Cut 1 from 10-count plastic canvas

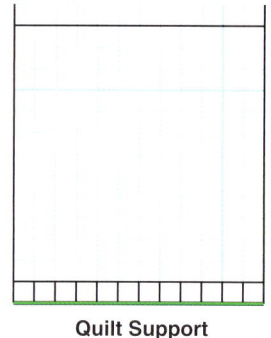

Quilt Support
12 holes x 14 holes
Cut 1 from white plastic canvas;
support will remain unstitched,
cut away blue lines

COLOR KEY	
Yards	**Worsted Weight Yarn**
4 (3.6m)	Uncoded areas on base are lime green Continental Stitches
	╱ Lime green Overcasting
	6-strand Embroidery Floss
7 (6.4m)	■ Black (12 strands)
6 (5.5m)	■ Red (12 strands)
5 (4.6m)	■ Medium pink (12 strands)
5 (4.6m)	■ Kelly green (12 strands)
5 (4.6m)	■ Lime green (12 strands)
1 (0.9m)	Medium brown (12 strands)

38 Main Street Village • The Needlecraft Shop • Berne, IN 46711 • NeedlecraftShop.com

Army-Navy Surplus Store

Size: 3¼ x inches W x 4 inches H x 3¼ inches D
(8.2cm x 10.2cm x 8.2cm)
Skill Level: Advanced

Materials

❏ Plastic canvas:
    1 sheet stiff 7-count
    Small amount clear 10-count
    Small amount clear 14-count
❏ Worsted weight yarn as listed in color key
❏ 6-strand cotton embroidery floss as listed in color key
❏ Clear sapphire blue beads:
    1 (6mm)
    2 (4mm)
❏ Sewing thread:
    White
    Chestnut
❏ Tapestry needles: #18 and #22
❏ Sharp sewing needle
❏ Hot-glue gun and glue stick

Stitching Step by Step

1 From stiff plastic canvas, cut all walls, bay window pieces, awning, roof pieces, shutters and base according to graphs.

2 From 10-count plastic canvas, cut bunting pieces according to graphs.

3 From 14-count plastic canvas, cut flag windows and signs according to graphs.

4 Stitch front wall according to graph; for right-side wall, reverse plastic canvas and stitch as a mirror image. Leave red dashed lines and the areas inside them unworked; the red lines are Whipstitching lines, and will be stitched during assembly. Using dark terra cotta yarn throughout, Overcast window openings on front and side walls, and Overcast top edges of front, side and door walls.

5 Stitch remaining walls, bay window pieces, awning, roof pieces, shutters and base, according to graphs, filling in uncoded areas on walls with chestnut Continental Stitches and uncoded areas on roof pieces with navy blue Continental Stitches. Again, leave red dashed lines unworked. Using terra cotta yarn, Overcast edges of main roof between arrows.

6 Using embroidery floss throughout, stitch flag windows, signs and buntings according to graphs, filling in uncoded areas on flag windows with light aqua Continental Stitches and uncoded areas on signs with white Continental Stitches. Overcast edges of buntings and signs as you stitch, continuing pattern of red, white and blue stripes on buntings.

7 Add embroidery stitches using floss as follows: navy blue—Straight Stitch around windows and awning stripes; navy blue (3 strands)—Backstitch lettering on signs; red (3 strands)—stripes on flags on flag windows; chestnut—Straight Stitch rectangles under windows on front and side walls, door handle on door wall, and outline door on left-side wall; French Knot doorknobs; tan—Straight Stitch outlines around remaining doors.

Assembly

1 Using dark terra cotta yarn throughout, Whipstitch long edges of bay window top, bottom and sides to front wall; Whipstitch top and bottom to sides along diagonal edges. Whipstitch bay window front to assembled window.

2 Repeat step 1 to add bay window to right-side wall.

3 Using sewing needle and chestnut thread, tack flag window insets behind window openings on front and side walls. Using sewing needle and white sewing thread, tack "Army–Navy" and "Surplus" signs to front and side walls as shown, centering them in the blocks of navy blue Continental Stitches.

4 Using sewing needle and white thread, tack bunting pieces where indicated on graphs near top of front, right side and door walls. Using royal blue floss, further secure buntings where indicated on graphs with vertical Straight Stitches.

5 Using white yarn, Overcast side and bottom edges of awning. Using navy blue yarn, Whipstitch top edge of awning to door wall above door, where indicated on graphs.

6 Using navy blue yarn throughout, Overcast side and bottom edges of shed roof; Whipstitch remaining edge of roof to side recessed corner wall along Whipstitching line.

7 Using chestnut yarn through step 9, Whipstitch side and back recessed corner walls together along edges Z, right sides facing; fold walls at a 90-degree angle with right sides facing inside.

8 Whipstitch back wall and side recessed corner wall together along vertical edges Y.

9 Whipstitch left side wall and back recessed corner wall together along vertical edges X.

10 Using tan yarn through step 11, Whipstitch bottom edges of front wall, door wall and side wall to base along Whipstitching lines. Whipstitch back wall and left side wall to edges of base.

11 Whipstitch back corner of shed together.

12 Using chestnut yarn throughout, Whipstitch remaining corners of building.

13 Position main roof on top of structure with unworked edges of roof matching unworked edges of back wall, recessed corner and left side wall. Using dark terra cotta yarn, Whipstitch roof to these pieces.

14 Secure diagonal edge of main roof to back of door wall using a small drop of hot glue.

15 Hot-glue shed roof to top edges of shed.

16 Using royal blue floss, sew 4mm beads to top edges of front and right side walls where indicated; sew 6mm bead to top of door wall.

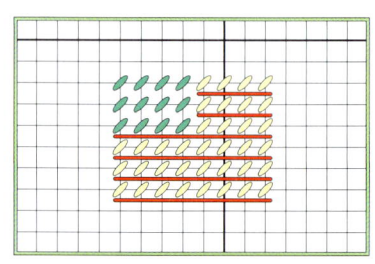

Army-Navy Surplus Flag Window
17 holes x 11 holes
Cut 2 from 14-count plastic canvas

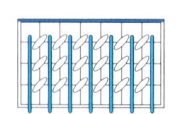

Army-Navy Surplus Awning
7 holes x 4 holes
Cut 1

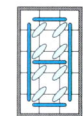

Army-Navy Surplus Bay Window Front/Sides
3 holes x 5 holes
Cut 6

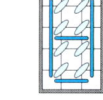

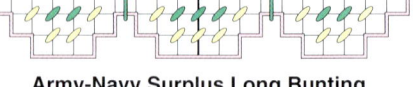

Army-Navy Surplus Long Bunting
20 holes x 3 holes
Cut 2 from 10-count plastic canvas

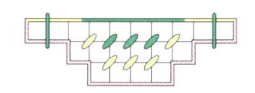

Army-Navy Surplus Short Bunting
10 holes x 3 holes
Cut 1 from 10-count plastic canvas

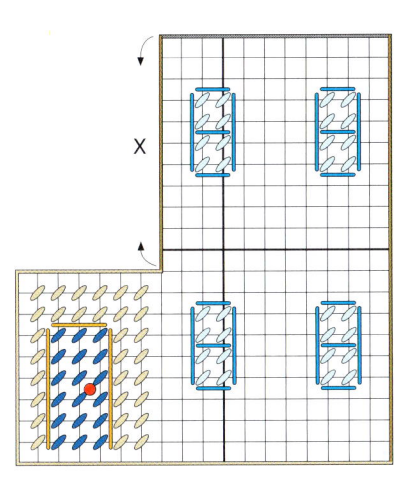

Army-Navy Surplus Left Side Wall
18 holes x 20 holes
Cut 1

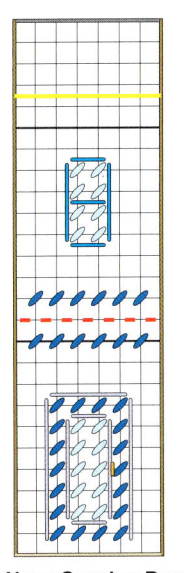

Army-Navy Surplus Door Wall
7 holes x 25 holes
Cut 1

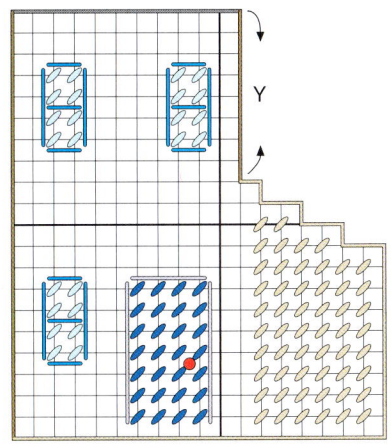

Army-Navy Surplus Back Wall
18 holes x 20 holes
Cut 1

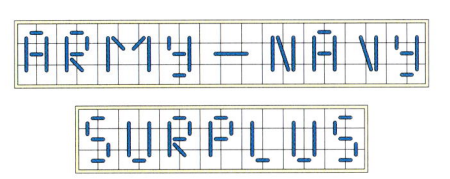

Army Navy Surplus Signs
20 holes x 3 holes
14 holes x 3 holes
Cut 1 of each from 14-count plastic canvas

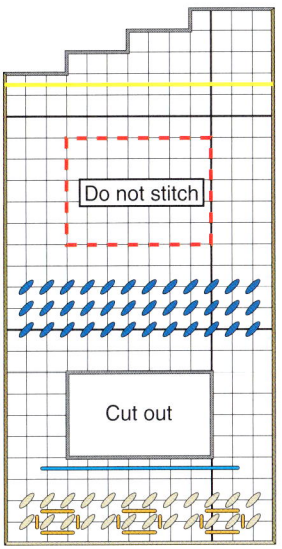

Army-Navy Surplus Right Side/Front Wall
13 holes x 25 holes
Cut 2
Stitch 1 as shown for front;
reverse 1 before stitching for right side wall

COLOR KEY		
Yards		**Worsted Weight Yarn**
30 (27.4m)	■	Chestnut
15 (13.7m)	■	Navy blue
10 (9.1m)	□	Tan
10 (9.1m)	■	Dark terra cotta
5 (4.7m)	■	Light gray
5 (4.7m)	□	Light aqua
2 (1.8m)	□	White
		Uncoded areas on door wall, back wall and left side wall are chestnut Continental Stitches
		Uncoded areas on roof pieces are navy blue Continental Stitches
	∕	Attach bunting with needle and thread
		6-strand Embroidery Floss
14 (12.8m)	□	White
6 (5.5m)	■	Royal blue
	∕	Royal blue Straight Stitch
		Uncoded areas on flag windows are light aqua (6-strand) Continental Stitches
4 (3.7m)	∕	Light aqua (6-strand) Overcasting
		Uncoded areas are White (6-strand) Continental Stitches
9 (8.2m)	∕	Navy blue (6-strand) Backstitch and Straight Stitch
	∕	Navy blue (3-strand) Backstitch and Straight Stitch
3 (2.7m)	∕	Chestnut Straight Stitch
2 (1.8m)	∕	Tan Straight Stitch
9 (8.2m)	∕	Red (6-strand) Backstitch and Straight Stitch
	∕	Red (3-strand) Backstitch, Straight Stitch and Overcasting
	∕	Dark terra cotta Straight Stitch
	●	Chestnut French Knot

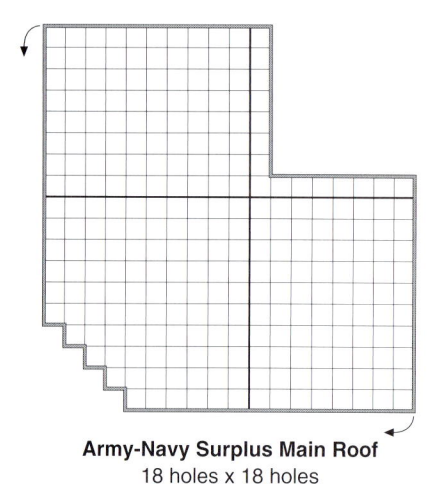

Army-Navy Surplus Main Roof
18 holes x 18 holes
Cut 1

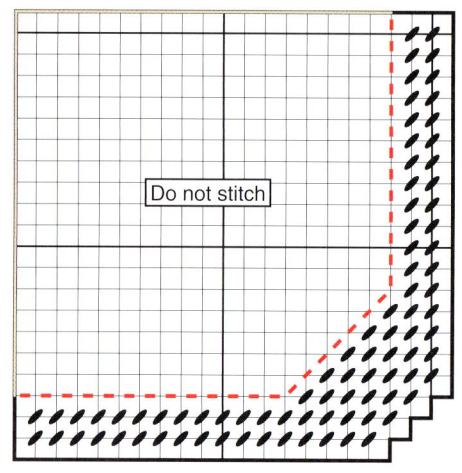

Army-Navy Surplus Base
21 holes x 21 holes
Cut 1

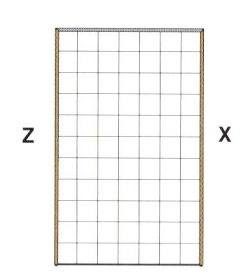

Army-Navy Surplus Back Recessed Corner Wall
7 holes x 11 holes
Cut 1

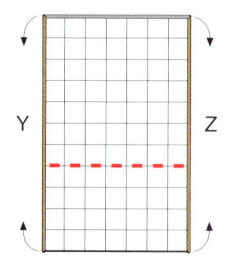

Army-Navy Surplus Side Recessed Corner Wall
7 holes x 11 holes
Cut 1

Army-Navy Surplus Bay Window Top/Bottom
5 holes x 2 holes
Cut 4

Army-Navy Surplus Shed Roof
7 holes x 9 holes
Cut 1

COLOR KEY	
Yards	**Worsted Weight Yarn**
30 (27.4m)	■ Chestnut
15 (13.7m)	■ Navy blue
10 (9.1m)	□ Tan
10 (9.1m)	■ Dark terra cotta
5 (4.7m)	■ Light gray
5 (4.7m)	□ Light aqua
2 (1.8m)	□ White
	Uncoded areas on door wall, back wall and left side wall are chestnut Continental Stitches
	Uncoded areas on roof pieces are navy blue Continental Stitches
	╱ Attach bunting with needle and thread
	6-strand Embroidery Floss
14 (12.8m)	□ White
6 (5.5m)	■ Royal blue
	╱ Royal blue Straight Stitch
	Uncoded areas on flag windows are light aqua (6-strand) Continental Stitches
4 (3.7m)	╱ Light aqua (6-strand) Overcasting
	Uncoded areas are White (6-strand) Continental Stitches
9 (8.2m)	╱ Navy blue (6-strand) Backstitch and Straight Stitch
	╱ Navy blue (3-strand) Backstitch and Straight Stitch
3 (2.7m)	╱ Chestnut Straight Stitch
2 (1.8m)	╱ Tan Straight Stitch
9 (8.2m)	╱ Red (6-strand) Backstitch and Straight Stitch
	╱ Red (3-strand) Backstitch, Straight Stitch and Overcasting
	╱ Dark terra cotta Straight Stitch
	● Chestnut French Knot

42 Main Street Village • The Needlecraft Shop • Berne, IN 46711 • NeedlecraftShop.com

Café

Size: 4¾ inches W x 5 inches H x 3½ inches D
(12.1cm x 12.7cm x 8.9cm)
Skill Level: Advanced

Materials

- Plastic canvas:
    1 sheet stiff 7-count
    Small amount black 7-count
    Small amount peach 7-count
    Small amount clear 14-count
- Worsted weight yarn as listed in color key
- 6-strand cotton embroidery floss as listed in color key
- 5½ inches (14cm) ⅜-inch (1cm) flat white lace
- 3 (1½-inch/3.8cm x ¾-inch/1.9cm) pieces white Venice lace
- Pompoms:
    8 (5mm) green
    4 (3mm) light green
- Chenille stems:
    3-inch green "bump" from bumpy chenille
    1½-inch (3.8cm) piece white iridescent
- 4 (1-inch) pieces black 22-gauge wire
- 2½-inch (6.4cm) square of black felt
- Sewing thread:
    White
    Black
- Tapestry needles: sizes #18 and #22
- Hand-sewing needle
- Hot-glue gun and glue stick

Stitching Step by Step

1. From stiff plastic canvas, cut all wall and roof pieces, awning and base according to graphs.

2. From black plastic canvas, cut sign bracket according to graph; it will remain unstitched.

3. From peach plastic canvas, cut coffee cup according to graph.

4. From 14-count plastic canvas, cut "Café" sign according to graph.

5. Stitch wall pieces according to graphs, filling in uncoded areas with peach Continental Stitches, and Overcasting window openings in side, awning side and front walls with periwinkle yarn. Leave red dashed lines unworked; these are Whipstitching lines, and will be stitched during assembly.

6 Stitch roof pieces according to graphs, noting that much of roof bottom remains unstitched; fill in remaining uncoded areas on roof top with light gray Continental Stitches and on roof sides with dark terra cotta Continental Stitches. As you stitch, Overcast edges of roof bottom with dark terra cotta yarn.

7 Stitch base according to graph, noting that area inside dashed red Whipstitching lines remains unstitched. Overcast edges of light spring green grass and camel front walk with adjacent colors.

8 Stitch awning in vertical rows according to graph, holding 20-gauge wire on underside along rows indicated by arrows on graph and catching wire under your stitches. Using grass green yarn, Overcast left edge of awning; using dark kelly green, Overcast right edge. Overcast bottom edge with adjacent colors to maintain the striped pattern. Bend finished awning slightly in a curved shape as shown in photo.

9 Fill in uncoded coffee cup with peach Continental Stitches, Overcasting edges as you stitch.

10 Using 12 strands white embroidery floss, fill uncoded area on sign with Continental Stitches and Overcast edges.

11 Cut flat lace into ½-inch-wide (1.3cm) pieces. Using sharp sewing needle and white thread, tack a piece along top edge in each window to resemble curtains.

12 Add embroidery stitches using yarn as follows: dark brown—Straight Stitch across top of coffee cup; dark terra cotta—Straight Stitch under first-floor windows and doors; grass green (1-ply)—Straight Stitch tops and sides of light periwinkle windows; gold—Straight Stitch handle on front door and French Knot doorknob on back door.

13 Add embroidery stitches using embroidery floss as follows: black—Straight Stitch windowpanes on periwinkle windows and outline doors; black (3 strands)—Backstitch lettering on sign; dark kelly green—Straight Stitch windowsills on roof windows.

14 Cut Venice lace to fit behind first-floor windows. Using sharp sewing needle and white thread, tack lace to back of stitched plastic canvas along top edge in each window to resemble curtains.

Assembly

1 Using peach yarn through step 2, Whipstitch top edge of awning to awning side wall where indicated on graph; Whipstitch long edge of bracket to side wall.

2 Whipstitch bottom edges of walls to base along Whipstitching lines, positioning awning side wall on left side and side wall on right side.

3 Trim felt to fit on unstitched floor inside café; using sharp sewing needle and black thread, tack felt to plastic canvas floor.

4 Using peach yarn, Whipstitch walls together along corners; Overcast top edges.

5 Using dark terra cotta yarn throughout, Whipstitch bottom edges of Mansard roof sides to roof bottom; loosely Whipstitch sides together at corners. Whipstitch roof top to sides.

Finishing

1 Cut green chenille bump in half; trim halves to resemble ½-inch (1.3cm) and 1-inch (2.5cm) evergreens. Hot-glue shorter tree to front right corner of base; hot-glue taller tree to base under awning.

2 Hot-glue three 5mm pompoms along each side of front walk; hot-glue remaining pompoms to base to suggest bushes.

3 Using 3 strands black floss and sharp sewing needle, form two tiny loops on back of sign; hang sign from bracket.

4 Center and hot-glue roof to walls.

5 Bend iridescent chenille stem to suggest steam; hot-glue to back of stitched coffee cup. Hot-glue bottom edge of coffee cup in center of roof.

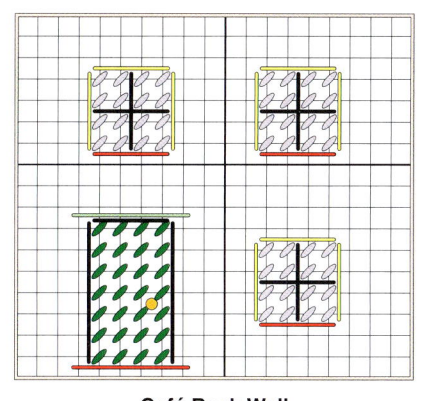

Café Back Wall
19 holes x 17 holes
Cut 1

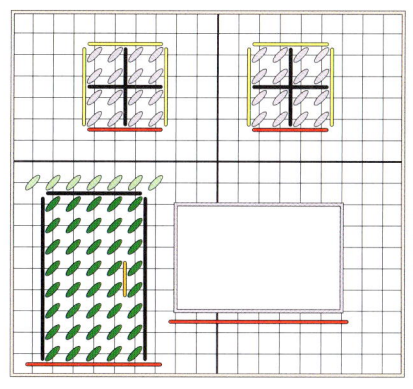

Café Front Wall
19 holes x 17 holes
Cut 1

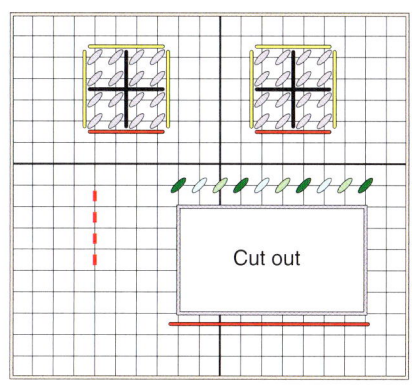

Café Side Wall
19 holes x 17 holes
Cut 1

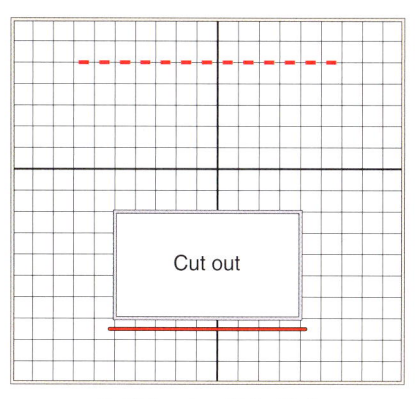

Café Awning Side Wall
19 holes x 17 holes
Cut 1

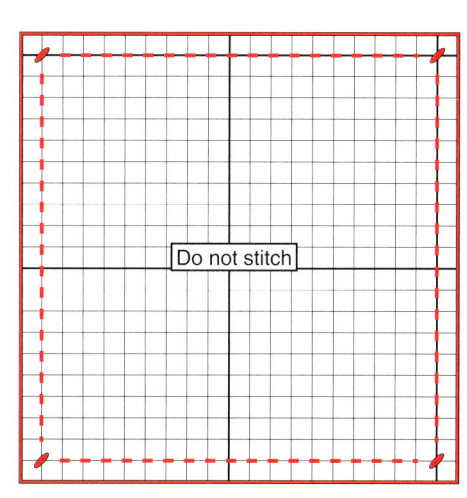

Café Mansard Roof Bottom
21 holes x 21 holes
Cut 1

COLOR KEY	
Yards	**Worsted Weight Yarn**
25 (22m)	■ Dark terra cotta
12 (11m)	□ Light periwinkle
9 (8.2m)	■ Light spring green
8 (7.3m)	■ Dark kelly green
4 (3.7m)	□ Light gray
3 (2.7m)	□ Bright green
3 (2.7m)	□ Grass green
2 (1.8m)	□ Camel
30 (27.4m)	Uncoded areas on walls and coffee cup are peach Continental Stitches
	╱ Peach Overcasting and Whipstitching
1 (0.9m)	╱ Dark brown Straight Stitch
	╱ Dark terra cotta Straight Stitch
1 (0.9m)	╱ Gold Straight Stitch
	╱ Dark kelly green Straight Stitch
	╱ Grass green (1-ply) Straight Stitch
	● Gold French Knot
	6-strand Embroidery Floss
6 (5.5m)	╱ Black (3-strand) Backstitch
	╱ Black Straight Stitch
2 (1.8m)	Uncoded areas on sign are white (12-strand) Continental Stitches
	╱ White (12-strand) Overcasting

The Needlecraft Shop • Berne, IN 46711 • NeedlecraftShop.com • **Main Street Village 45**

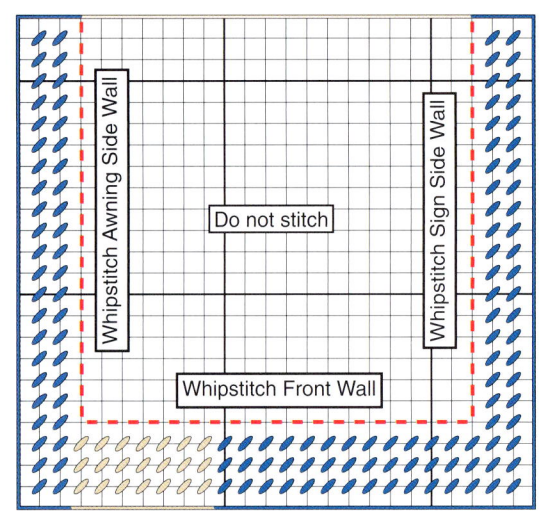

Café Base
25 holes x 23 holes
Cut 1

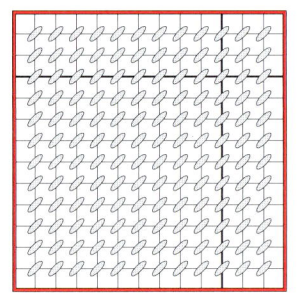

Café Mansard Roof Top
13 holes x 13 holes
Cut 1

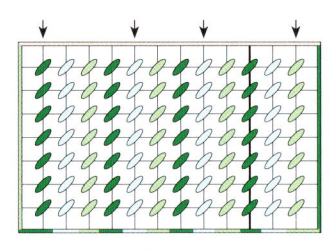

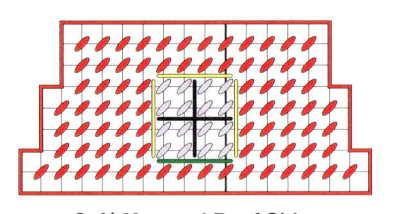

Café Mansard Roof Sides
17 holes x 8 holes
Cut 4

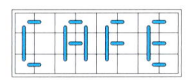

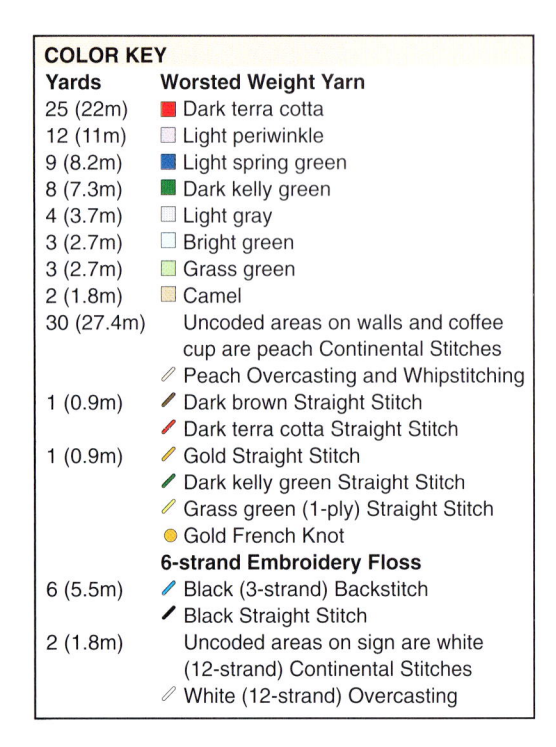

Café Awning
13 holes x 8 holes
Cut 1

Café Sign
8 holes x 3 holes
Cut 1 from 14-count plastic canvas

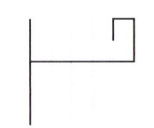

Café Sign Bracket
5 holes x 5 holes
Cut 1 from black plastic canvas;
do not stitch,
cut away blue lines

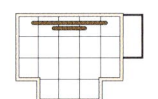

Café Coffee Cup
6 holes x 4 holes
Cut 1 from peach plastic canvas

COLOR KEY		
Yards		**Worsted Weight Yarn**
25 (22m)	■	Dark terra cotta
12 (11m)	□	Light periwinkle
9 (8.2m)	■	Light spring green
8 (7.3m)	■	Dark kelly green
4 (3.7m)	□	Light gray
3 (2.7m)	□	Bright green
3 (2.7m)	□	Grass green
2 (1.8m)	□	Camel
30 (27.4m)		Uncoded areas on walls and coffee cup are peach Continental Stitches
	∕	Peach Overcasting and Whipstitching
1 (0.9m)	∕	Dark brown Straight Stitch
	∕	Dark terra cotta Straight Stitch
1 (0.9m)	∕	Gold Straight Stitch
	∕	Dark kelly green Straight Stitch
	∕	Grass green (1-ply) Straight Stitch
	●	Gold French Knot
		6-strand Embroidery Floss
6 (5.5m)	∕	Black (3-strand) Backstitch
	∕	Black Straight Stitch
2 (1.8m)		Uncoded areas on sign are white (12-strand) Continental Stitches
	∕	White (12-strand) Overcasting

46 Main Street Village • The Needlecraft Shop • Berne, IN 46711 • NeedlecraftShop.com

Ladies' Apparel Shop

Size: 3½ inches W x 5¼ inches H x 3¾ inches D
(8.9cm x 13.3cm x 9.5cm)
Skill Level: Advanced

Materials

- Plastic canvas:
    - 1 sheet stiff 7-count
    - Small amount white 7-count
    - Small amount clear 10-count
    - Small amount clear 14-count
- Worsted weight yarn as listed in color key
- 6-strand cotton embroidery floss as listed in color key
- 5 inches (½-inch) white flat scallop-edge lace
- 24 (3mm) pearl beads
- Snippet of green feather
- Sewing thread:
    - Medium gold
    - Green
    - White
- Tapestry needles: sizes #18 and #22
- Sewing needle
- Hot-glue gun and glue stick

Stitching Step by Step

Building

1. From stiff plastic canvas, cut all wall pieces, loggia ceiling and base according to graphs.

2. Stitch plastic canvas according to graphs, filling in uncoded areas on walls with medium gold Continental Stitches and noting that much of base remains unstitched. For now, wrap only the two center pillars with white yarn. Leave red dashed lines unworked; these are Whipstitching lines, and will be stitched during assembly.

3. Overcast openings for windows and top edges of all walls *except* lower floor front wall using dark gold.

4. Add embroidery stitches using yarn as follows: dark slate blue (1 ply)—Straight Stitch windows and doors; white—Backstitch front doorknob and French Knot back doorknob; grass green—Straight Stitch greenery.

5. Add embroidery stitches using floss as follows: kelly green—Lazy Daisy Stitch leaves in flower boxes; red—French Knot flowers in window boxes.

Friezes

1. From stiff plastic canvas, cut frieze pieces according to graphs.

2. Stitch pieces according to graphs, Overcasting edges as you stitch.

The Needlecraft Shop • Berne, IN 46711 • NeedlecraftShop.com • **Main Street Village 47**

3 Using sewing needle and white thread, stitch pearl beads to stitched friezes according to graphs.

4 Cut scallop-edge lace as long as plastic canvas frieze pieces; hot-glue lace behind plastic canvas so that scalloped edge is visible along bottom.

Windows

1 From 10-count plastic canvas, cut window insets according to graphs.

2 Stitch window insets according to graphs, using 12 strands cotton embroidery floss throughout and filling in uncoded areas with white Continental Stitches; Overcast edges with 12 strands white embroidery floss as you stitch.

3 Add embroidery stitches to windows using 6 strands floss as follows: black—Backstitch neckline and French Knot buttons on pink dress; lavender—Straight Stitch details on purple sweater; light blue—Straight Stitch belt on blue dress; lime green—Straight Stitch band on hat; sienna—Straight Stitch stands on purple sweater and hat insets.

4 Center insets behind window openings in side and lower floor front walls; using sewing needle and gold thread, tack insets behind window openings.

5 Cut a tiny snippet from green feather; using sewing needle and green thread, stitch feather to hat as desired.

Sign

1 From 14-count canvas, cut apparel shop sign according to graph.

2 Using 6 strands light gold embroidery floss, fill in uncoded areas on sign with Continental Stitches; Overcast edges as you stitch.

3 Embroider sign using 3 strands of floss throughout: sienna—Backstitch lettering; kelly green—Lazy Daisy Stitch leaf; pink—French Knot flower.

Chimneys

1 From stiff plastic canvas, cut all chimney pieces according to graphs.

2 Stitch all chimney pieces according to graphs. Using dark terra cotta yarn throughout, Whipstitch front, back, short and long sides of second-floor chimney together, with top edges even; Overcast edges. Whipstitch all pieces of first-floor chimney together; Overcast edges.

Roofs

1 From stiff plastic canvas, cut all roof pieces according to graphs.

2 From white plastic canvas, cut roof trims and brackets according to graphs; they will remain unstitched.

3 Stitch roof pieces according to graphs, filling in uncoded areas with dark slate blue Continental Stitches and Overcasting edges of lower level roof and main roof as you stitch. Leave red dashed Whipstitching lines unworked for now.

4 Using dark slate blue yarn throughout, Whipstitch shorter sides of mansard roof front and back to matching opposite edges of mansard roof top. Whipstitch mansard roof sides to remaining opposite edges of roof top. Whipstitch front, back and sides together at corners to give mansard roof its shape; Overcast edges.

5 Using white thread and sewing needle, tack white roof railings to edges on top of mansard roof; hot-glue assembled roof in center of main roof.

Assembly

1 Using white yarn throughout, Whipstitch bottom edge of lower floor front wall to base where indicated by red dashed line. Whipstitch front edge of loggia ceiling to *back* of upper floor front wall with right side of ceiling facing down.

2 Using tan yarn, Whipstitch lower edge of upper floor front wall to front edge of base.

3 Using white yarn throughout, Whipstitch loggia ceiling to walls along remaining adjacent edges.

4 Using grass green and tan yarns according to graphs, Whipstitch lower edges of side walls to edges of base.

5 Using white yarn through step 6, Whipstitch inner edges of front wall and loggia ceiling to adjacent edges of side walls.

6 Working from the top down, wrap corner columns snugly, but not so tight as to buckle or warp the plastic canvas; secure yarn ends on underside of base.

7 Using white and grass green yarns according to graphs, Whipstitch upper and lower back walls to edges of side walls and base.

8 Using sewing needle and white thread, tack white brackets along top edge of front wall where indicated by red lines on graph. Make sure top edge of brackets is even with top edge of wall.

9 Center and hot-glue lower level roof onto back of shop as shown; hot-glue first-floor chimney to roof.

10 Hot-glue main roof to top of shop so that front edge of roof is even with front edge of brackets. Center and hot-glue assembled mansard roof on top of main roof; hot-glue roof to top edges of brackets. Hot-glue chimney to left side of mansard roof as shown.

11 Hot-glue friezes to front and sides of shop so that lace edge hangs below ceiling. Hot-glue sign to center of front frieze as shown.

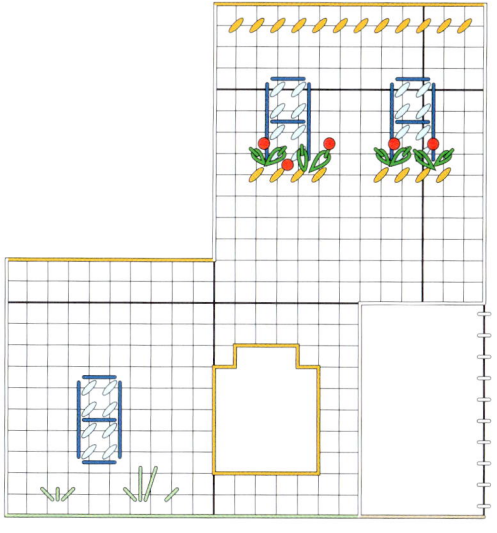

Apparel Shop Left Side Wall
23 holes x 24 holes
Cut 1

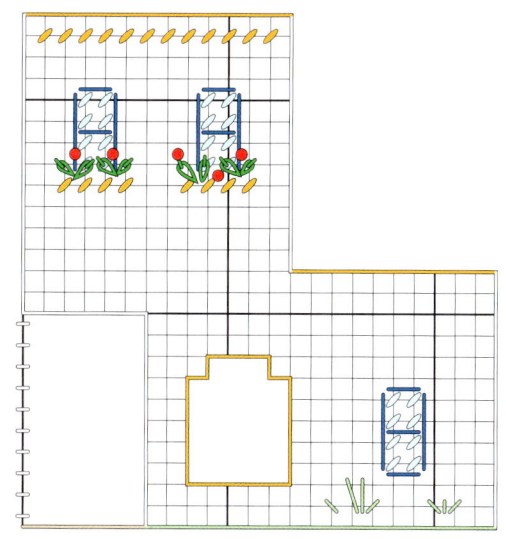

Apparel Shop Right Side Wall
23 holes x 24 holes
Cut 1

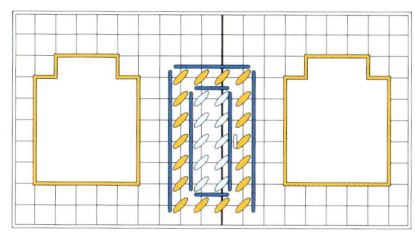

Apparel Shop Lower Floor Front Wall
19 holes x 10 holes
Cut 1

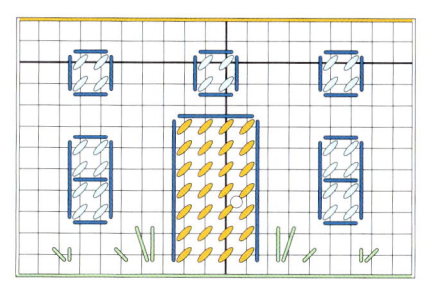

Apparel Shop Lower Floor Back Wall
19 holes x 12 holes
Cut 1

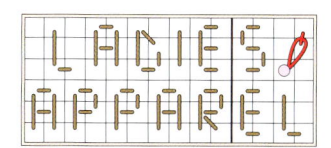

Apparel Shop Sign
14 holes x 6 holes
Cut 1 from 14-count plastic canvas

COLOR KEY

Yards	Worsted Weight Yarn
12 (11m)	■ Dark gold
14 (12.8m)	□ White
5 (4.6m)	□ Light aqua
4 (3.7m)	■ Dark terra cotta
3 (2.7m)	□ Tan
20 (18.3m)	Uncoded areas on walls are medium gold Continental Stitches
22 (20.1m)	Uncoded areas on roof pieces are dark slate blue Continental Stitches
3 (2.7m)	⁄ Grass green Straight Stitch
	⁄ Light gold Overcasting
	⁄ Dark slate blue (1-ply) Backstitch and Straight Stitch
	○ White French Knot
	⁄ White Backstitch
	— Attach bracket
	○ Attach pearl bead

6-strand Embroidery Floss

Yards	
2 (1.8m)	■ Royal blue (12-strand)
2 (1.8m)	□ Bright pink (12-strand)
2 (1.8m)	■ Purple (12-strand)
2 (1.8m)	■ Black (12-stitch)
8 (7.3m)	Uncoded areas on windows are white (12-strand) Continental Stitch
3 (2.7m)	Uncoded area on sign is light gold Continental Stitches
	⁄ White (12-strand) Overcasting
	⁄ Light gold (3-strand) Overcasting
1 (0.9m)	⁄ Sienna Backstitch (3-strand)
1 (0.9m)	⁄ Sienna Backstitch (6-strand)
1 (0.9m)	⁄ Lavender Straight Stitch
1 (0.9m)	⁄ Light blue Straight Stitch
	⁄ Lime green Straight Stitch
	⁄ Black Straight Stitch
5 (4.6m)	❧ Kelly green (3-strand) Lazy Daisy Stitch
	❧ Kelly green (6-strand) Lazy Daisy Stitch
3 (2.7m)	● Red French Knot
	○ Bright pink French Knot (3-strand)
	● Black French Knot

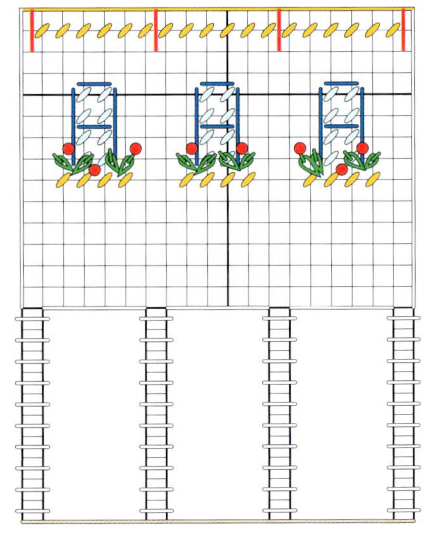

Apparel Shop Upper Floor Front Wall
19 holes x 24 holes
Cut 1

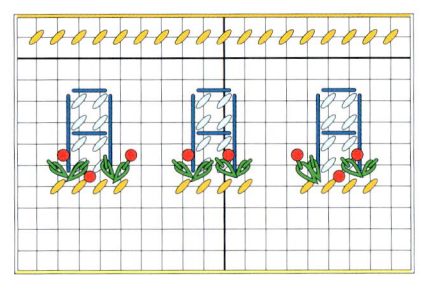

Apparel Shop Upper Floor Back Wall
19 holes x 12 holes
Cut 1

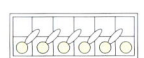

Side Frieze
6 holes x 2 holes
Cut 2

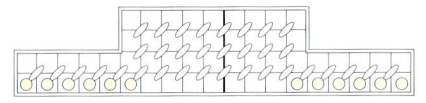

Front Frieze
19 holes x 4 holes
Cut 1

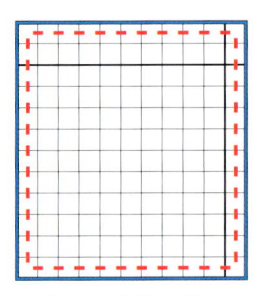

Mansard Roof Top
11 holes x 12 holes
Cut 1

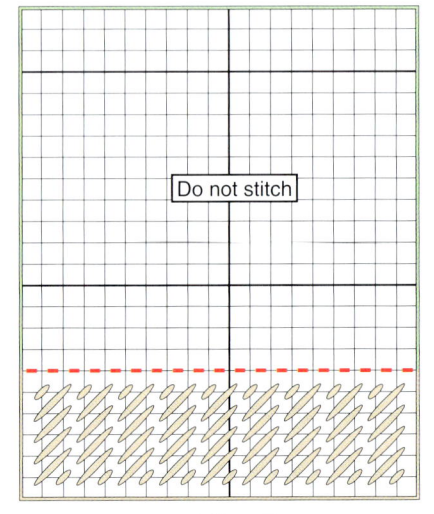

Do not stitch

Apparel Shop Base
19 holes x 23 holes
Cut 1

COLOR KEY	
Yards	**Worsted Weight Yarn**
12 (11m)	Dark gold
14 (12.8m)	White
5 (4.6m)	Light aqua
4 (3.7m)	Dark terra cotta
3 (2.7m)	Tan
20 (18.3m)	Uncoded areas on walls are medium gold Continental Stitches
22 (20.1m)	Uncoded areas on roof pieces are dark slate blue Continental Stitches
3 (2.7m)	Grass green Straight Stitch
	Light gold Overcasting
	Dark slate blue (1-ply) Backstitch and Straight Stitch
	White French Knot
	White Backstitch
	Attach bracket
	Attach pearl bead
	6-strand Embroidery Floss
2 (1.8m)	Royal blue (12-strand)
2 (1.8m)	Bright pink (12-strand)
2 (1.8m)	Purple (12-strand)
2 (1.8m)	Black (12-stitch)
8 (7.3m)	Uncoded areas on windows are white (12-strand) Continental Stitch
3 (2.7m)	Uncoded area on sign is light gold Continental Stitches
	White (12-strand) Overcasting
	Light gold (3-strand) Overcasting
1 (0.9m)	Sienna Backstitch (3-strand)
1 (0.9m)	Sienna Backstitch (6-strand)
1 (0.9m)	Lavender Straight Stitch
1 (0.9m)	Light blue Straight Stitch
	Lime green Straight Stitch
	Black Straight Stitch
5 (4.6m)	Kelly green (3-strand) Lazy Daisy Stitch
	Kelly green (6-strand) Lazy Daisy Stitch
3 (2.7m)	Red French Knot
	Bright pink French Knot (3-strand)
	Black French Knot

Main Street Village • The Needlecraft Shop • Berne, IN 46711 • NeedlecraftShop.com

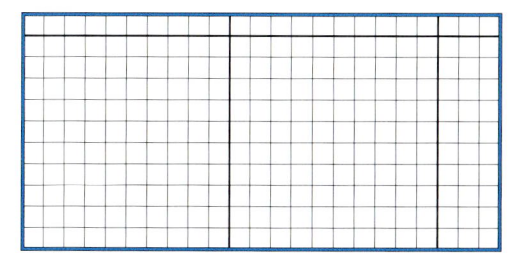

Apparel Shop Lower Level Roof
23 holes x 11 holes
Cut 1

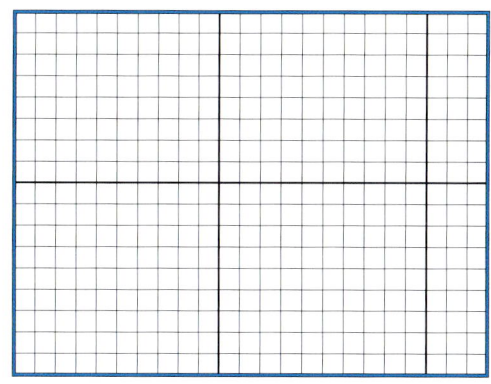

Apparel Shop Main Roof
23 holes x 17 holes
Cut 1

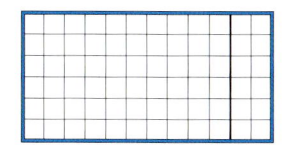

Mansard Roof Side
12 holes x 6 holes
Cut 2

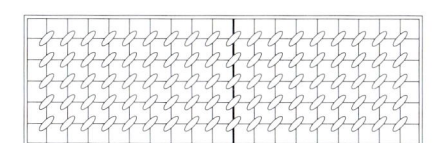

Apparel Shop Loggia Ceiling
19 holes x 6 holes
Cut 1

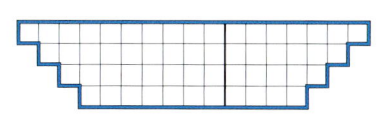

Mansard Roof Front/Back
17 holes x 4 holes
Cut 2

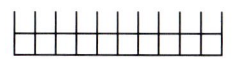

Short Roof Railing
10 holes x 2 holes
Cut 2 from white plastic canvas

Apparel Shop Bracket
2 holes x 2 holes
Cut 4 from white plastic canvas;
they will remain unstitched,
cut away blue lines

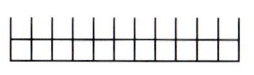

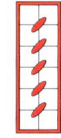

Second-Floor Chimney Long Side
2 holes x 6 holes
Cut 1

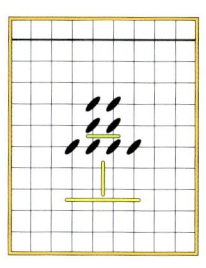

Long Roof Railing
11 holes x 2 holes
Cut 2 from white plastic canvas

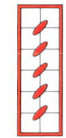

First-Floor Chimney
2 holes x 6 holes
Cut 4

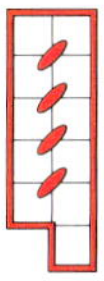

Hat Window
9 holes x 11 holes
Cut 1 from 10-count plastic canvas

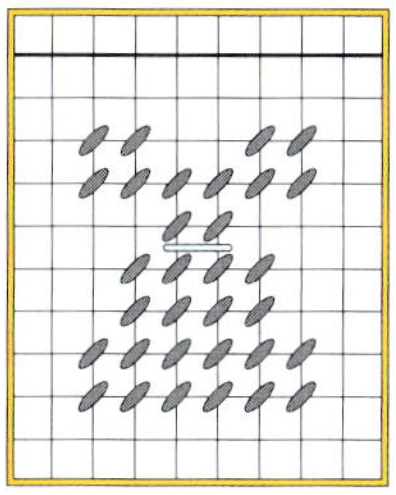

Blue Dress Window
9 holes x 11 holes
Cut 1 from 10-count plastic canvas

Second-Floor Chimney Front/Back
2 holes x 6 holes
Cut 2, reverse one before stitching

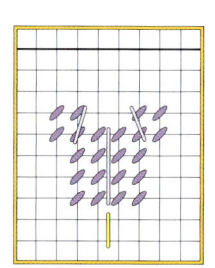

Purple Sweater Window
9 holes x 11 holes
Cut 1 from 10-count plastic canvas

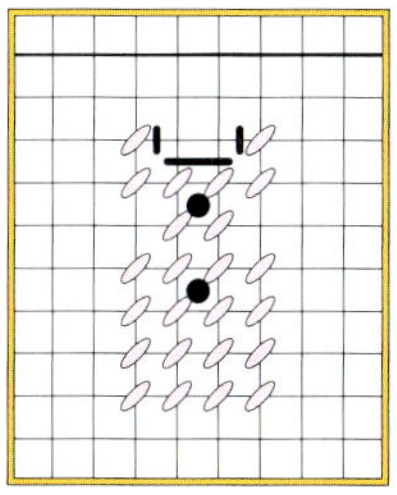

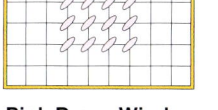

Pink Dress Window
9 holes x 11 holes
Cut 1 from 10-count plastic canvas

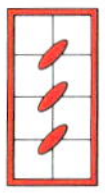

Second-Floor Chimney Short Side
2 holes x 4 holes
Cut 1

The Needlecraft Shop • Berne, IN 46711 • NeedlecraftShop.com • *Main Street Village* 51

Sweet Shop

Size: 2¾ inches W x 3¾ inches H x 4¼ inches D
(7cm x 9.5cm x 10.8cm)
Skill Level: Advanced

Materials

- Plastic canvas:
    - 1 sheet stiff 7-count
    - Small amount pink 7-count
    - Small amount clear 10-count
    - Small amount clear 14-count
- Worsted weight yarn as listed in color key
- 6-strand cotton embroidery floss as listed in color key
- 1 yard white iridescent craft cord
- ⅜-inch-wide flat lace:
    - 2 (¾-inch/1.9cm) pieces
    - 1½-inch (3.2cm) piece
- ½ inch (1.3cm) x ½-inch (1.3cm) heart-shaped motif cut from white Venice lace
- Beads:
    - 2 (4mm) opaque red faceted
    - 2 (4mm) clear faceted
    - 2 white plastic craft beads
    - ½-inch (1.3cm) x ½-inch (1.3cm) silver onion-dome or melon-shaped bead
- Sewing thread:
    - White
    - Brown
    - Cornflower blue
    - Pink
- Tapestry needles: #18 and #22
- Sewing needle
- Hot-glue gun and glue stick

Stitching Step by Step

1 From stiff plastic canvas, cut all walls, awning pieces, door, shutters, roof and base according to graphs.

2 From pink plastic canvas, cut two awning brackets according to graphs; they will remain unstitched.

3 From 10-count plastic canvas, cut one sign according to graph.

4 From 14-count plastic canvas, cut one window inset according to graph.

5 Stitch walls according to graphs, filling in uncoded areas on walls with medium brown Continental Stitch, and filling in uncoded area on sign side wall with light blue Continental Stitch. Leave red dashed lines unworked; these are Whipstitching lines, and will be stitched during assembly. Overcast window openings and bottom edge of door opening with medium brown yarn; Overcast top and left side of door opening with bright pink yarn.

6 Stitch door, shutters, roof and base according to graphs, noting that most of base remains unstitched; using light gray yarn, Overcast edges adjacent to light gray stitching. Overcast top, bottom and left side edges of door with bright pink yarn; Overcast top, bottom and one side edge of each shutter with cornflower blue yarn; Overcast edges of roof with camel yarn.

7 Stitch awning top and front according to graphs. Whipstitch awning pieces together along matching long edges, using alternating bright pink and dark pink stitches to maintain striped pattern. Overcast side and bottom (scalloped) edges using bright pink yarn.

8 Stitch "Sweets" sign according to graph using 12 strands floss, filling in uncoded areas with white Continental Stitches. Overcast edges with light blue floss.

9 Using 6 strands light blue floss, fill in uncoded area of window inset with Continental Stitches; Overcast edges as you stitch.

10 Add embroidered details using embroidery floss as follows: dark brown—Backstitch lettering on "Sweets" sign and wall; dark brown (3-ply)—Backstitch lettering on window inset; dark brown (12-ply)—French Knot "bullets" on sign on wall; red—French Knots on sign; cornflower blue—Straight Stitch around light blue stitching and outline windows; dark blue—Straight Stitch and Backstitch soda glass; dark brown—Straight Stitch tree trunks, door and door handle.

11 Using iridescent craft cord, work French Knot "bubbles" at top of soda glass.

12 Add embroidered details using yarn as follows: medium brown—French Knot doorknob on front door; red—French knot cherry atop soda; grass green—French Knot tree tops on window side wall.

13 *Soda straw:* Separate 1 ply each from red and white yarn; thread both pieces onto #18 needle. Bring needle up at one end of straw; twist yarn until colors spiral. Take yarn back down through other end of straw; secure on back.

14 *Candy sticks on "Sweets" sign:* Thread 6-strand pieces of red and white embroidery floss onto #22 needle. Bring needle up at one end of candy stick; twist floss until colors spiral. Take floss back down through other end of candy stick; secure floss on back. Repeat to add second candy stick.

Assembly

1 Using cornflower blue yarn, Whipstitch vertical arms of awning brackets to front wall above door and window along vertical Whipstitching lines. Using bright pink yarn, Whipstitch unfinished edge of awning to front wall along horizontal dashed red Whipstitching line. Bend awning down to rest on diagonal arm of brackets; using sewing needle and pink thread, tack edges of awning to brackets.

2 Using bright pink yarn, Whipstitch door to opening in front wall along right edge.

3 Using sewing needle and white thread, tack flat lace to stitched window inset, positioning edge of lace about 2 rows above "Try Our" lettering. Center window inset behind opening in front wall; using sewing needle and brown thread, tack window inset to back of front wall.

4 Using sewing needle and white thread, tack flat lace to stitched window inset, positioning edge of lace about 2 rows above "Try Our" lettering. Center window inset behind opening in front wall; using sewing needle and brown thread, tack window inset to back of front wall.

5 Using sewing needle and white thread, tack ¾-inch (1.9cm) piece of flat lace at top edge of each remaining window to suggest curtains; trim lace as needed.

6 Using sewing needle and cornflower blue thread, stitch red bead to center of each shutter; using dark pink yarn, Whipstitch shutters beside window.

7 Using cornflower blue yarn, Whipstitch bottom edge of front wall to base where indicated. Using medium brown yarn throughout, Whipstitch bottom edges of remaining walls to base. Using cornflower blue and brown yarns according to graphs, Whipstitch walls together up corners.

8 Bring sewing needle threaded with white thread up through roof at blue dot; thread on silver onion-dome bead, then one clear bead; go back down through silver bead in same hole and tighten thread. Bring needle back up through roof at red dot; thread on two white plastic craft beads, then clear bead; go back down through white beads in same hole and tighten thread. Secure thread ends to hold beads in place.

9 Position roof inside walls, aligning roof edges with second row of stitches. Using sewing needle and brown thread, tack roof to sweet shop, using a small amount of hot-glue to secure roof to back of front wall.

10 Hot glue lace heart to front door; hot-glue sign above awning.

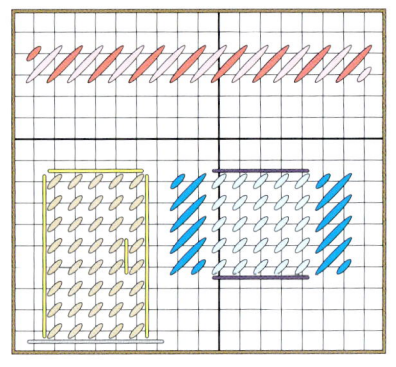

Sweet Shop Back Wall
18 holes x 16 holes
Cut 1

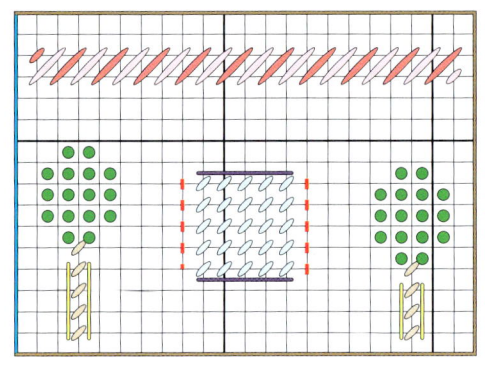

Sweet Shop Window Side Wall
22 holes x 16 holes
Cut 1

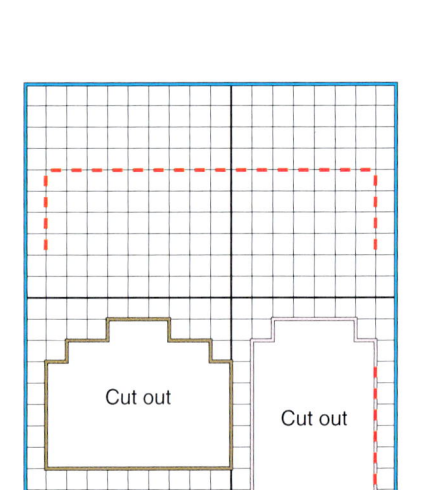

Sweet Shop Front Wall
18 holes x 20 holes
Cut 1

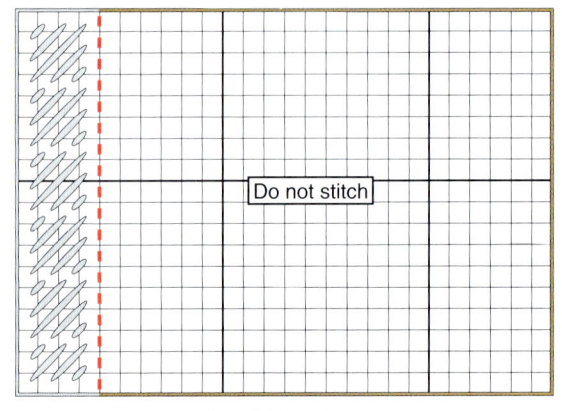

Sweet Shop Base
26 holes x 18 holes
Cut 1

COLOR KEY		
Yards		**Worsted Weight Yarn**
10 (9.1m)	■	Cornflower blue
8 (7.3m)	□	Camel
7 (6.4m)	□	Bright pink
6 (5.5m)	□	Light blue
5 (4.6m)	■	Dark pink
3 (2.7m)	□	Light gray
1 (0.9m)		White
20 (18.3m)		Uncoded areas on walls are medium brown Continental Stitch
	∕	Medium brown Overcasting
	∕	Striped Straight Stitch (4 ply each red and white)
1 (0.9m)	●	Red French Knot
2 (1.8m)	●	Grass green French Knot
	●	Medium brown French Knot
		6-strand Embroidery Floss
8 (7.3m)		Uncoded areas on sweet shop sign are white (12-strand) Continental Stitches
7 (6.4m)	□	Light blue
6 (5.5m)		Uncoded areas on window inset are light blue Continental Stitches
	∕	Dark brown Backstitch and Straight Stitch
	∕	Dark brown (3-strand) Backstitch and Straight Stitch
	∕	Striped Straight Stitch (6 strands each red and white)
3 (2.7m)	∕	Cornflower blue Straight Stitch
2 (1.8m)	∕	Dark blue Straight Stitch
1 (0.9m)	■	Dark gold (12-strand)
1 (0.9m)	■	Medium pink (12-strand)
1 (0.9m)	○	Red French Knot
	○	Dark brown (12-strand) French Knot
		Craft Cord
1 (0.9m)	○	White iridescent French Knot

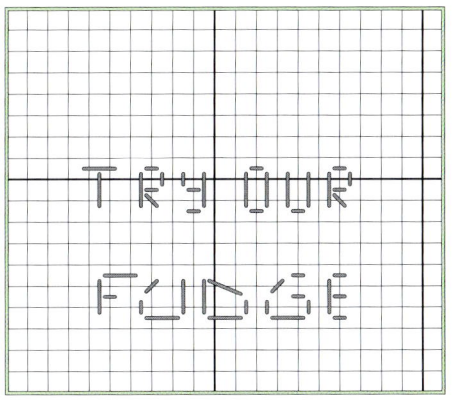

Front Window Inset
21 holes x 18 holes
Cut 1 from 14-count plastic canvas

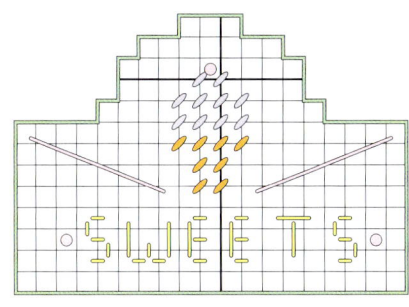

Sweet Shop Sign
19 holes x 13 holes
Cut 1 from 10-count plastic canvas

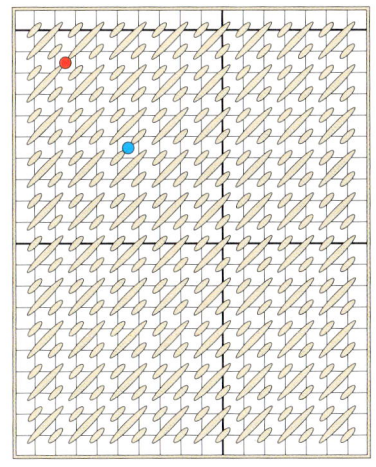

Sweet Shop Roof
17 holes x 21 holes
Cut 1

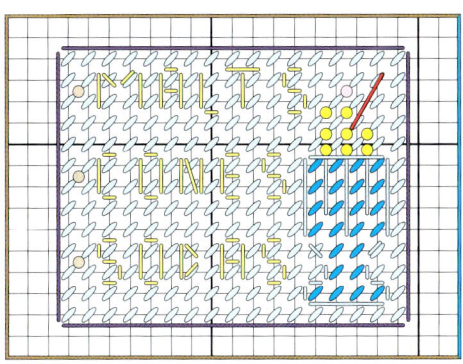

Sweet Shop Sign Side Wall
22 holes x 16 holes
Cut 1

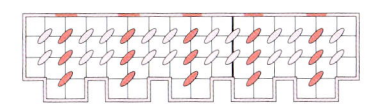

Sweet Shop Awning Front
16 holes x 4 holes
Cut 1

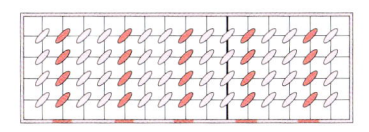

Sweet Shop Awning Top
16 holes x 5 holes
Cut 1

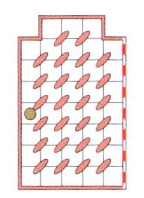

Sweet Shop Door
5 holes x 8 holes
Cut 1

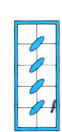

Sweet Shop Shutter
2 holes x 5 holes
Cut 2

Sweet Shop Awning Bracket
4 holes x 3 holes
Cut 2 from pink plastic canvas;
do not stitch,
cut away blue lines

The Needlecraft Shop • Berne, IN 46711 • NeedlecraftShop.com • **Main Street Village 55**

Bookstore

Size: 3½ inches W x 4⅜ inches H x 3⅛ inches D
(8.9cm x 11.9cm x 7.9cm)
Skill Level: Intermediate

Materials

- Plastic canvas:
    1 sheet stiff 7-count
    Small amount black 7-count
    Small amount clear 10-count
- Worsted weight yarn as listed in color key
- 6-strand cotton embroidery floss as listed in color key
- 2 (6mm) clear faceted beads
- 6 (5mm) grass green pompoms
- 8 inches clay colored ribbon with small print
- Sewing thread:
    Medium brown
    Black
- Tapestry needles: #18 and #22
- Sewing needle
- Hot-glue gun and glue stick

Stitching Step by Step

1 From stiff plastic canvas, cut all walls, door, base, dormer windows and roof pieces according to graphs.

2 From black plastic canvas, cut lamp brackets according to graphs.

3 From 10-count plastic canvas, cut window insets and "Books" sign according to graphs.

4 Stitch all walls, door, base, dormers and all roof pieces according to graphs, noting that much of the base will remain unstitched, and filling in uncoded areas with bone Continental Stitch. Reverse two dormer window roofs before you stitch. Leave red dashed lines unworked; these are Whipstitching lines, and will be stitched during assembly.

5 Using bone yarn throughout, Whipstitch two dormer sides to each dormer front so that diagonal edges of dormer sides are on bottom; Overcast remaining edges.

6 Overcast window openings in walls using medium brown yarn. Overcast top and right edges of opening for door in front wall using medium clay yarn. Overcast top, bottom and right side edges of front door using brick red yarn.

56 Main Street Village • The Needlecraft Shop • Berne, IN 46711 • NeedlecraftShop.com

7 Using 12 strands cotton embroidery floss throughout, stitch sign and window insets, Overcasting edges as you stitch, and filling in uncoded areas with white Continental Stitches.

8 Add embroidery stitches using yarn as follows: camel—Straight Stitch timber details on upper story and outline around back door; medium brown—Straight Stitch around camel areas on walls and around first-story window on back wall.

9 Add embroidery stitches using 6-strand cotton embroidery floss as follows: camel—Straight Stitch around windows on front door and dormers, and French Knot door knobs; medium gold—Backstitch book details on window insets; dark brown—Straight Stitch lettering on sign.

Assembly

1 Using medium clay yarn, Whipstitch front door to left edge of door opening.

2 Using sewing needle and medium brown thread, tack window insets behind openings in front and side walls.

3 Using sewing needle and black thread, stitch long arms of lamp brackets beside doorway as shown in photo.

4 Using light clay yarn, Whipstitch bottom edge of front wall to base. Using grass green yarn throughout, Whipstitch side and back walls to base; complete grass green and light gray Overcasting around front of base. Using camel yarn throughout, Whipstitch walls together at corners, working from bottom up; Overcast top edges.

5 Using hunter green yarn throughout, Whipstitch roof pieces together along one long edge; Overcast remaining edges. Whipstitch dormer window roof pieces together in matching pairs along one straight edge with diagonal edges facing to back; Overcast remaining edges.

6 Hot-glue roof to top of bookstore; hot-glue dormers to roof. Hot-glue dormer roofs to dormers.

7 Hot-glue sign to front wall over bone Continental Stitches. Hot-glue faceted beads on ends of brackets for lamps. Hot-glue lengths of ribbon around middle of building, gluing on individual motifs cut from ribbon as desired. Glue pompoms to base of bookstore as shown, for bushes.

COLOR KEY

Yards	Worsted Weight Yarn
20 (18.3m)	■ Hunter green
16 (4.6m)	■ Camel
8 (7.3m)	□ Light clay
7 (6.4m)	□ Light aqua
6 (5.5m)	■ Medium brown
6 (5.5m)	□ Medium clay
5 (4.6m)	■ Grass green
3 (2.7m)	■ Brick red
2 (1.8m)	□ Light gray
20 (18.3m)	Uncoded areas on walls and dormers are bone Continental Stitches
	⁄ Bone Whipstitch
	⁄ Camel Straight Stitch
	⁄ Medium brown Straight Stitch

	6-strand Embroidery Floss
12 (11m)	Uncoded areas on sign and window insets are white (12-strand) Continental Stitches
	⁄ White (12-strand) Overcasting
2 (1.8m)	■ Cornflower blue (12-strand)
2 (1.8m)	■ Lime green (12-strand)
1 (0.9m)	■ Dark red (12-strand)
2 (1.8m)	⁄ Camel Straight Stitch
2 (1.8m)	⁄ Dark brown Backstitch and Straight Stitch
1 (0.9m)	⁄ Medium gold Backstitch
2 (1.8m)	○ Camel French Knot

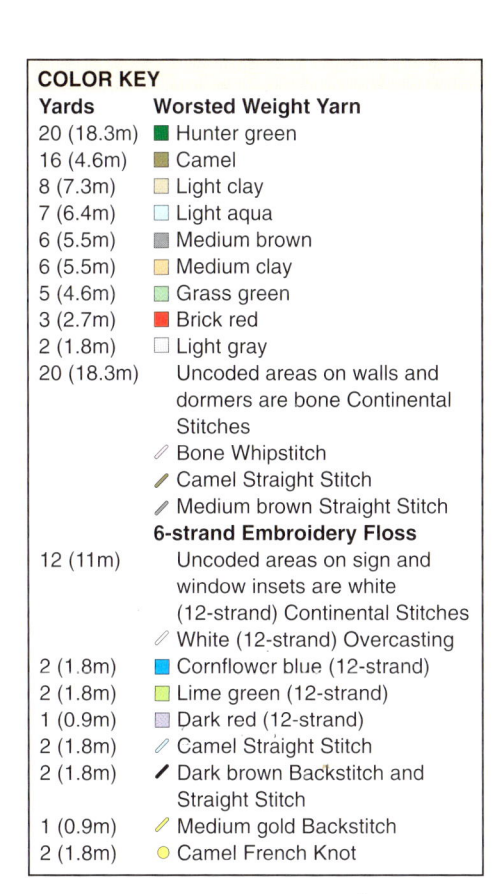

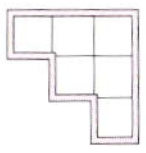

Bookstore Dormer Window Side
3 holes x 3 holes
Cut 4; reverse 2 before stitching

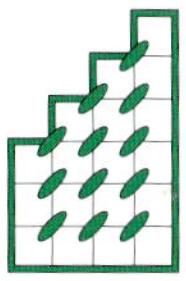

Bookstore Dormer Window Roof
4 holes x 6 holes
Cut 4; reverse 2 before stitching

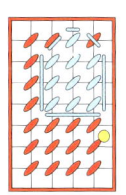

Bookstore Door
5 holes x 8 holes
Cut 1

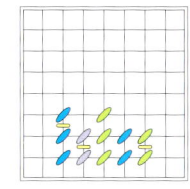

Bookstore Window Inset
8 holes x 8 holes
Cut 4 from 10-count plastic canvas

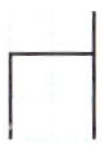

Bookstore Lamp Bracket
2 holes x 3 holes
Cut 2 from black plastic canvas, cut away blue lines

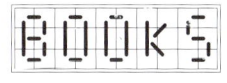

Bookstore Sign
10 holes x 3 holes
Cut 1 from 10-count plastic canvas

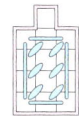

Bookstore Dormer Window Front
3 holes x 5 holes
Cut 2

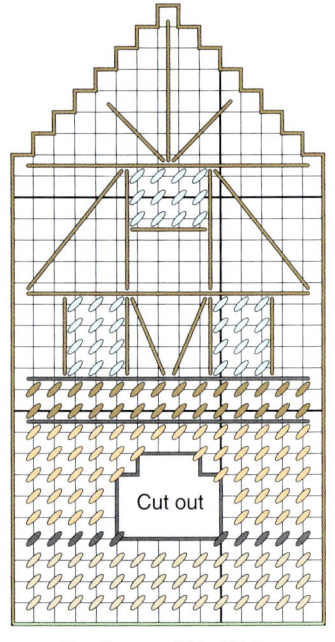

Bookstore Side Walls
15 holes x 29 holes
Cut 2

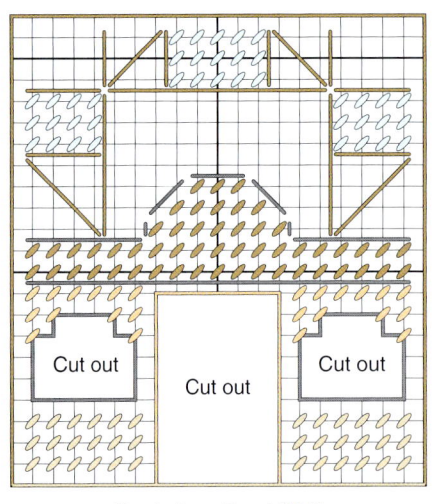

Bookstore Front Wall
20 holes x 22 holes
Cut 1

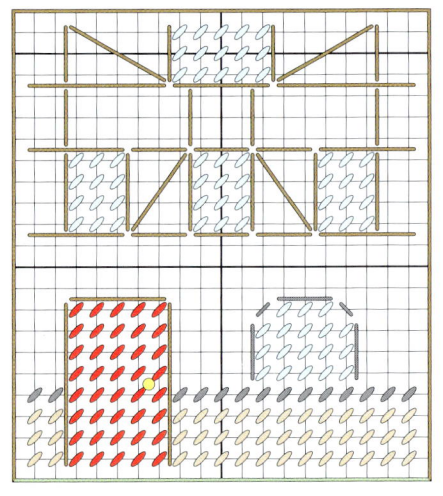

Bookstore Back Wall
20 holes x 22 holes
Cut 1

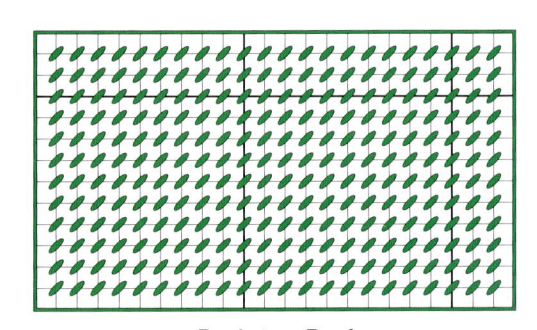

Bookstore Roof
23 holes x 13 holes
Cut 2

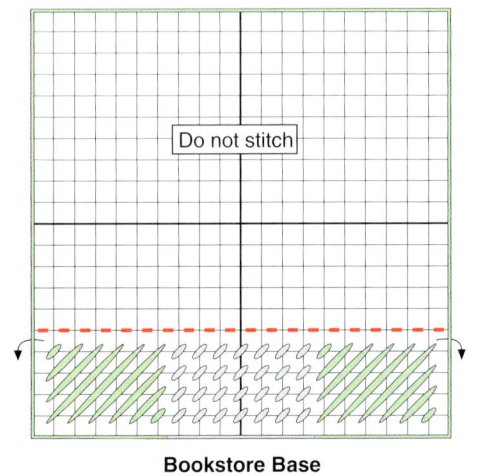

COLOR KEY		
Yards	**Worsted Weight Yarn**	
20 (18.3m)	■	Hunter green
16 (4.6m)	■	Camel
8 (7.3m)	□	Light clay
7 (6.4m)	□	Light aqua
6 (5.5m)	■	Medium brown
6 (5.5m)	■	Medium clay
5 (4.6m)	□	Grass green
3 (2.7m)	■	Brick red
2 (1.8m)	□	Light gray
20 (18.3m)		Uncoded areas on walls and dormers are bone Continental Stitches
	⁄	Bone Whipstitch
	⁄	Camel Straight Stitch
	⁄	Medium brown Straight Stitch
	6-strand Embroidery Floss	
12 (11m)		Uncoded areas on sign and window insets are white (12-strand) Continental Stitches
	⁄	White (12-strand) Overcasting
2 (1.8m)	■	Cornflower blue (12-strand)
2 (1.8m)	■	Lime green (12-strand)
1 (0.9m)	■	Dark red (12-strand)
2 (1.8m)	⁄	Camel Straight Stitch
2 (1.8m)	⁄	Dark brown Backstitch and Straight Stitch
1 (0.9m)	⁄	Medium gold Backstitch
2 (1.8m)	○	Camel French Knot

Bookstore Base
20 holes x 20 holes
Cut 1

58 *Main Street Village* • *The Needlecraft Shop* • *Berne, IN 46711* • *NeedlecraftShop.com*

Flower Shop

Size: 4 inches W x 4⅜ inches H x 4 inches D
(10.2cm x 11.1cm x 10.2cm)
Skill Level: Advanced

Materials

- Plastic canvas:
    1 sheet stiff 7-count
    Small amount sea green 7-count
    Small amount clear 10-count
- Worsted weight yarn as listed in color key
- 6-strand cotton embroidery floss as listed in color key
- 3 (6mm) opaque jade faceted beads
- White sewing thread
- Tapestry needles: #18 and #22
- Sewing needle
- Hot-glue gun and glue stick

Stitching Step by Step

1 From stiff plastic canvas, cut all walls, roof, stairway landing, balcony floor, door, recessed walls, bay window sides, top and front, base and ceiling pieces according to graphs.

2 From sea green plastic canvas, cut stairs, front and back stairway rail/supports, and balcony side and front railings according to graphs; they will remain unstitched.

3 From 10-count plastic canvas, cut window insets and "Flowers" sign pieces according to graphs.

4 Stitch all walls according to graphs, filling in uncoded areas with dark terra cotta Continental Stitches, and Overcasting window openings with jade yarn. Leave red dashed lines unworked; these are Whipstitching lines, and will be stitched during assembly.

5 Stitch roof, stairway landing, balcony floor, front door and recessed wall and ceiling pieces according to graphs, filling in uncoded areas with dark terra cotta Continental Stitches. Overcast edges of roof with light clay yarn.

6 Stitch base according to graph, noting that most of it will remain unstitched; Overcast edge adjacent to stitching with light clay yarn.

7 Stitch bay window pieces according to graphs, stitching sides as mirror images and filling in uncoded areas with light clay Continental Stitches; Overcast opening in bay window front with jade yarn.

8 Using 12 strands embroidery floss, stitch flower sign and window insets according to graphs, filling in uncoded areas on sign with white Continental Stitches and uncoded areas on window insets with pale yellow Continental Stitches; Overcast edges with adjacent colors.

9 Add embroidery stitches using jade yarn as follows: Straight Stitch around very pale yellow windows, side and back doors, and between wall colors on main walls; French Knots on bay window.

10 Add embroidery stitches using 6-strand cotton embroidery floss as follows: dark brown—Straight Stitch windowpanes and lettering on sign, and French Knot doorknobs; jade—Straight Stitch details on walls and front door; purple, red and orange—French Knot flowers on window insets; leaf green (3-strand)—Straight Stitch flower leaves in window insets; red (12-strand)—Cross Stitch on top of front wall; kelly green—Lazy Daisy Stitches beside red Cross Stitch.

Assembly
Front Wall, Balcony & Doorway

1 Using sewing needle and white thread, center and tack front window insets behind openings in front windows.

2 Using light clay yarn, Whipstitch long edge of balcony floor along Whipstitching line on front wall. Using sea green yarn throughout, Whipstitch balcony side railings to front wall as shown on photo; Whipstitch bottom edges of side and front railings to balcony floor.

3 Using light clay yarn, Whipstitch bottom edges of door and recessed walls to base around area of light clay stitching, right sides facing inward.

4 Using dark terra cotta yarn throughout, Whipstitch recessed walls and door together along corners. Lay recessed ceiling right side down atop recessed walls and door; Whipstitch ceiling to top edges of recessed walls and door.

5 Position flower shop front wall along front edge of base, aligning opening with recessed doorway; using sea green yarn, Whipstitch front wall to recessed doorway up sides and across top. Using dark terra cotta yarn, Whipstitch bottom edge of front wall to base.

Bay Window Side Wall

1 Using sea green yarn throughout, Whipstitch bay window sides and top to bay window side wall along Whipstitching lines.

2 Using sewing needle and white thread, center and tack bay window inset behind opening in bay window. Using sea green yarn, Whipstitch bay window front to sides and top, folding in sides as needed to match diagonal edges of top. Whipstitch bay window sides to top along diagonal edges.

3 Position assembled bay window wall along left edge of base, matching bottom of bay window with protruding edges of base. Using dark terra cotta yarn, Whipstitch bottom edge of bay window wall, including bay window, to base.

Stairway & Stairway Side Wall

1 Using jade yarn throughout, Whipstitch back stairway rail/support along vertical Whipstitching line near right end of stairway side wall.

2 Whipstitch one short end of stairway landing to one short end of stairs. Stairs and landing will rest against surface of wall, with landing at top. Overcast long edge A (inner edge) of stairs; Whipstitch adjacent long edge of landing to wall along horizontal Whipstitcht top of stairs (below door).

3 Whipstitch remaining short (back) edge of stairway landing to back stairway rail/support, matching edges B.

4 Lay front stairway rail/support over stairs and landing, matching edges C, D and E; Whipstitch pieces together along matching edges, wrapping yarn around post C.

5 Overcast top edges of front and back railing/supports, and bottom edge of back railing/support; Overcast bottom rung of stairs, tacking inner corner of bottom stair to wall at yellow dot on graph.

6 Using dark terra cotta yarn, Whipstitch bottom edge of stairway side wall to base (stairs will protrude beyond base).

Remaining Walls

1 Using dark terra cotta yarn, Whipstitch bottom edge of back wall to back edge of base.

2 Using sea green yarn, Whipstitch side walls to front wall at corners; using dark terra cotta yarn, Whipstitch side walls to back wall at corners.

Roof

1 Using light clay yarn throughout, Overcast one short end of roof; this will be front edge of roof.

2 Position roof atop flower shop with Overcast edge behind front wall. Using light clay yarn, Whipstitch roof to side and back walls.

Finishing

1 Using jade yarn, Overcast top edges of front wall.

2 Using jade floss, sew beads to top edge of front wall where indicated.

3 Hot-glue top edge of sign to front edge of balcony so that it hangs over doorway.

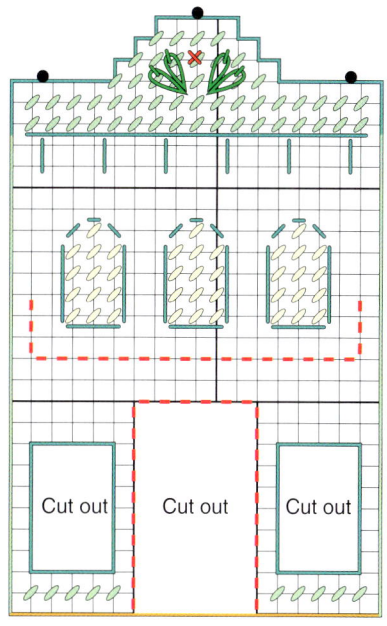

Flower Shop Front Wall
18 holes x 28 holes
Cut 1

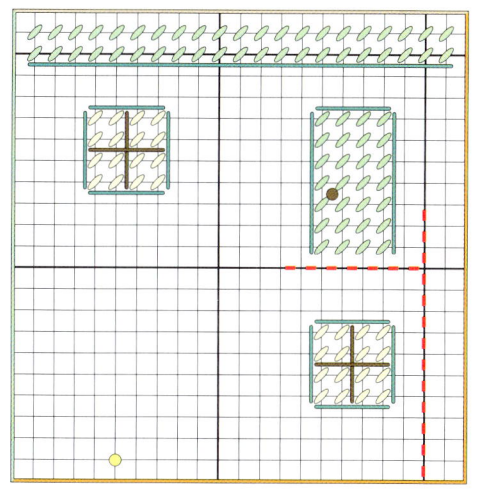

Flower Shop Stairway Side Wall
22 holes x 22 holes
Cut 1

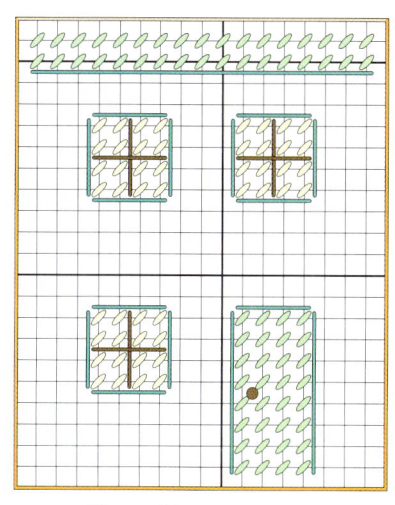

Flower Shop Back Wall
18 holes x 22 holes
Cut 1

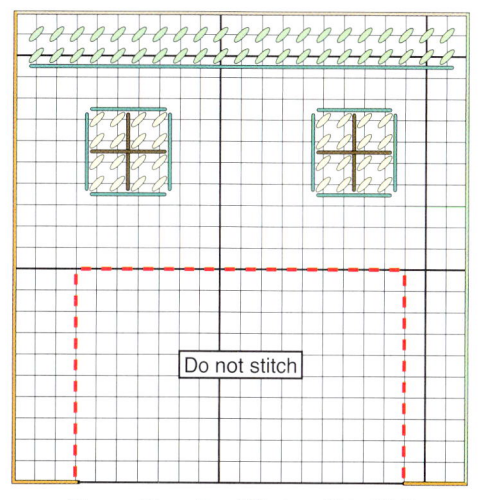

Flower Shop Bay Window Side Wall
22 holes x 22 holes
Cut 1

COLOR KEY		
Yards		**Worsted Weight Yarn**
18 (16.5m)	☐	Sea green
10 (9.1m)	☐	Jade
10 (9.1m)	☐	Light clay
7 (6.4m)	☐	Very pale yellow
25 (22.9m)		Uncoded areas on walls are dark terra cotta Continental Stitches
	╱	Dark terra cotta Whipstitching
	╱	Jade Backstitch and Straight Stitch
	●	Jade French Knot
	●	Attach bead
		6-strand Embroidery Floss
10 (9.1m)		Uncoded areas on window insets are very pale yellow (12-strand) Continental Stitches
5 (4.6m)	╱	Dark brown Backstitch and Straight Stitch
4 (3.7m)	╱	Jade Straight Stitch
3 (2.7m)		Uncoded area on sign is white (12-strand) Continental Stitches
2 (1.8m)	☐	Taupe (12-strand)
2 (1.8m)	☐	Red (12-strand)
2 (1.8m)	●	Orange French Knot
2 (1.8m)	●	Purple French Knot
1 (0.9m)	🌿	Kelly green Lazy Daisy Stitch
1 (0.9m)	╱	Leaf green (3-strand) Straight Stitch
	●	Red French Knot
	●	Dark brown French Knot
	╱	White Overcasting
	╱	Very pale yellow Overcasting

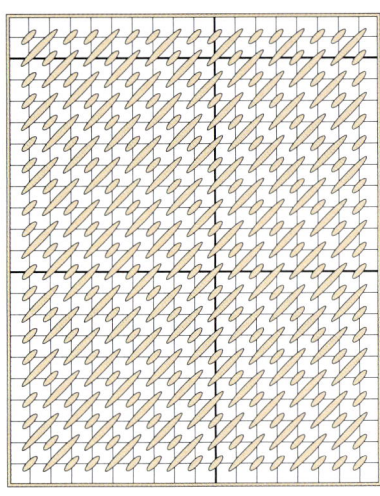

Flower Shop Roof
18 holes x 22 holes
Cut 1

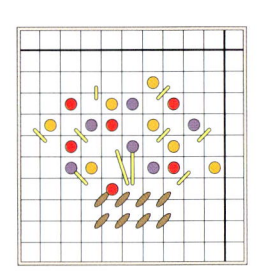

Flower Shop Bay Window Inset
11 holes x 11 holes
Cut 1 from 10-count plastic canvas

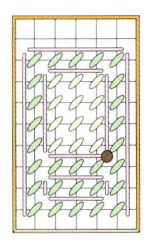

Flower Shop Front Door
6 holes x 10 holes
Cut 1

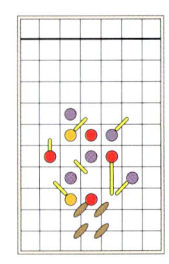

Flower Shop Front Window Inset
7 holes x 11 holes
Cut 2 from 10-count plastic canvas

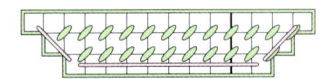

Bay Window Top
14 holes x 3 holes
Cut 1

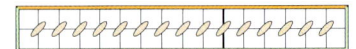

Flower Shop Balcony Floor
16 holes x 2 holes
Cut 1

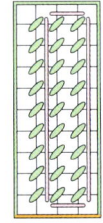

Bay Window Sides
4 holes x 10 holes
Cut 2
Work as mirror images

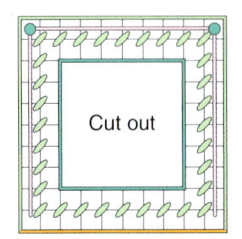

Bay Window Front
10 holes x 10 holes
Cut 1

Cut out

COLOR KEY	
Yards	Worsted Weight Yarn
18 (16.5m)	Sea green
10 (9.1m)	Jade
10 (9.1m)	Light clay
7 (6.4m)	Very pale yellow
25 (22.9m)	Uncoded areas on walls are dark terra cotta Continental Stitches
	Dark terra cotta Whipstitching
	Jade Backstitch and Straight Stitch
	Jade French Knot
	Attach bead
	6-strand Embroidery Floss
10 (9.1m)	Uncoded areas on window insets are very pale yellow (12-strand) Continental Stitches
5 (4.6m)	Dark brown Backstitch and Straight Stitch
4 (3.7m)	Jade Straight Stitch
3 (2.7m)	Uncoded area on sign is white (12-strand) Continental Stitches
2 (1.8m)	Taupe (12-strand)
2 (1.8m)	Red (12-strand)
2 (1.8m)	Orange French Knot
2 (1.8m)	Purple French Knot
1 (0.9m)	Kelly green Lazy Daisy Stitch
1 (0.9m)	Leaf green (3-strand) Straight Stitch
	Red French Knot
	Dark brown French Knot
	White Overcasting
	Very pale yellow Overcasting

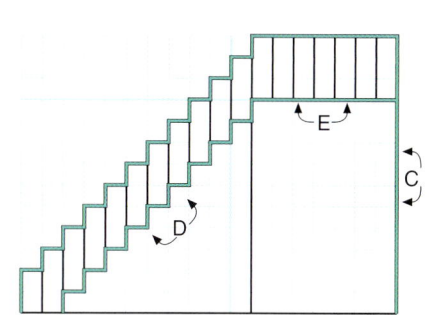

Front Stairway Rail/Support
18 holes x 13 holes
Cut 1 from sea green plastic canvas,
cut away blue lines

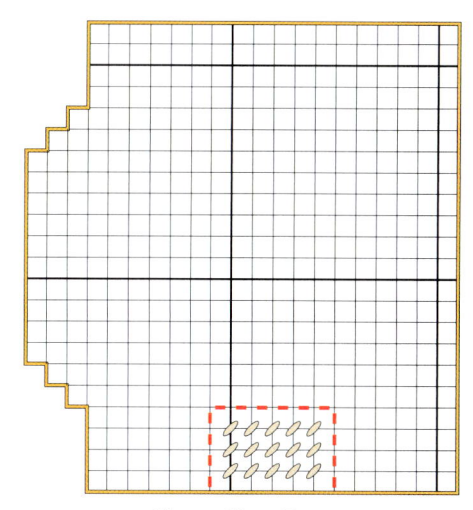

Flower Shop Base
21 holes x 22 holes
Cut 1

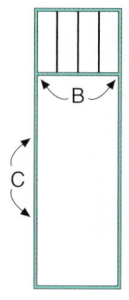

Back Stairway Rail/Support
4 holes x 13 holes
Cut 1 from sea green plastic canvas,
cut away blue lines

Flower Shop Balcony Side Railing
2 holes x 3 holes
Cut 2 from sea green plastic canvas,
cut away blue lines

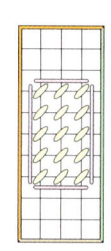

Flower Shop Recessed Wall
4 holes x 10 holes
Cut 2
Stitch 1 as shown for right-hand wall;
reverse Whipstitch colors on side edges
for left-hand wall

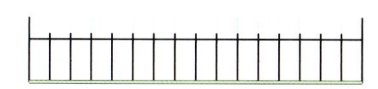

Flower Shop Balcony Front Railing
16 holes x 3 holes
Cut 1 from sea green plastic canvas,
cut away blue lines

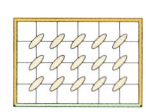

Flower Shop Recessed Ceiling
6 holes x 4 holes
Cut 1

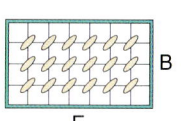

Stairway Landing
7 holes x 4 holes
Cut 1

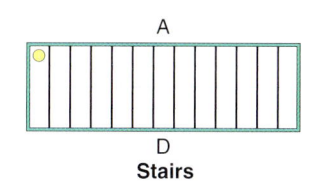

Stairs
13 holes x 4 holes
Cut 1 from sea green plastic canvas,
cut away blue lines

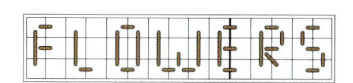

Flower Shop Sign
15 holes x 3 holes
Cut 1 from 10-count plastic canvas

The Needlecraft Shop

306 E. Parr Road
Berne, IN 46711
www.NeedlecraftShop.com
© 2005 The Needlecraft Shop

The full line of The Needlecraft Shop products is carried by Annie's Attic catalog.

TOLL-FREE ORDER LINE
or to request a free catalog
(800) 582-6643
Customer Service
(800) 449-0440
Fax (800) 882-6643
Visit www.AnniesAttic.com

We have made every effort to ensure the accuracy and completeness of these instructions. We cannot, however, be responsible for human error, typographical mistakes or variations in individual work. Reprinting or duplicating the information, photographs or graphics in this publication by any means, including copy machine, computer scanning, digital photography, e-mail, personal Web site and fax, is illegal. Failure to abide by federal copyright laws may result in litigation and fines.

ISBN: 1-57367-214-9
All rights reserved.
Printed in USA
1 2 3 4 5 6 7 8 9

Shopping for Supplies

For supplies, first shop your local craft and needlework stores. Some supplies may be found in fabric, hardware and discount stores. If you are unable to find the supplies you need, please call Annie's Attic at (800) 259-4000 to request a free catalog that sells plastic canvas supplies.

Getting Started

Before You Cut

Buy one brand of canvas for each entire project, as brands can differ slightly in the distance between bars. Count holes carefully from the graph before you cut, using the bolder lines that show each 10 holes. These 10-mesh lines begin in the lower left corner of each graph to make counting easier. Mark canvas before cutting, then remove all marks completely before stitching. If the piece is cut in a rectangular or square shape and is either not worked, or worked with only one color and one type of stitch, we do not include the graph in the pattern. Instead, we give the cutting and stitching instructions in the general instructions or with the individual project instructions.

Covering the Canvas

Bring needle up from back of work, leaving a short length of yarn on back of canvas; work over short length to secure. To end a thread, weave needle and thread through the wrong side of your last few stitches; clip. Follow the numbers on the small graphs beside each stitch illustration; bring your needle up from the back of the work on odd numbers and down through the front of the work on even numbers. Work embroidery stitches last, after the canvas has been completely covered by the needlepoint stitches.

Basic Stitches

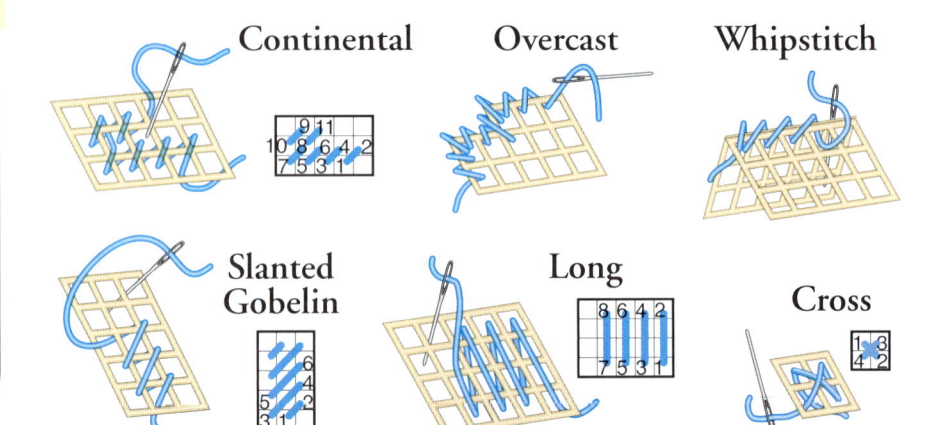

Continental Overcast Whipstitch

Slanted Gobelin Long Cross

Embroidery Stitches

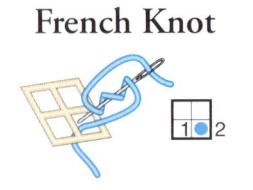

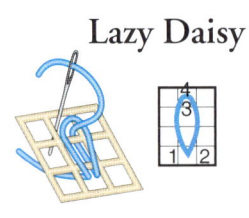

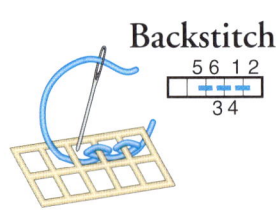

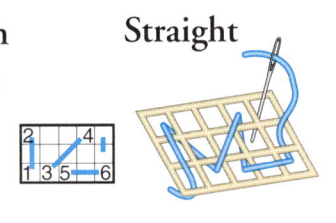

French Knot Lazy Daisy Backstitch Straight

METRIC KEY:
millimeters = (mm)
centimeters = (cm)
meters = (m)
grams = (g)

64 **Main Street Village** • The Needlecraft Shop • Berne, IN 46711 • NeedlecraftShop.com